AF600401

THE CATHOLIC UNIVERSITY OF AMERICA
CANON LAW STUDIES
No. 105

CUSTOM

AN HISTORICAL SYNOPSIS AND COMMENTARY

A DISSERTATION

Submitted to the Faculty of Canon Law of the Catholic University of America in Partial Fulfillment of the Requirements for the Degree of

DOCTOR OF CANON LAW

BY

REV. MERLIN JOSEPH GUILFOYLE, J.C.L.
Priest of the Archdiocese of San Francisco

THE CATHOLIC UNIVERSITY OF AMERICA
WASHINGTON, D. C.
1937

Nihil Obstat:

VALENTINUS T. SCHAAF, O.F.M., J.C.D.,
Censor Deputatus.

Washingtonii, D. C., die XVII Maii, 1937.

Imprimatur:

JOANNES J. MITTY, D.D.,
Archiepiscopus Sancti Francisci.

die XXIX Maii, 1937.

Printed by
THE PAULIST PRESS
New York, N. Y.

TO MY FATHER AND MY MOTHER

TABLE OF CONTENTS

CHAPTER III

CHAPTER IV

PART II

CHAPTER VI

COMMENTARY ON THE LEGISLATION OF THE CODE

PAGE

FOREWORD

At first sight it seems paradoxical that a society, such as the Church, should have in its legal system a place for custom, while nearly all the modern civil governments, even democracies, have more or less suppressed customary law. A second thought, however, will show that in many ways custom is even befitting the character of the Church.

Through custom is shown the unity between members and head in the Church. Indeed it has become a principle that the acts of the people in custom are the best *interpreter* of the law.

Through custom a Church, which is world-wide and intended for all peoples, insinuates its government like the action of leaven into the mass of every time and place. Of necessity there are not enough laws to provide for a society so immense. Custom, however, forms laws. When the legislator does not act, custom may *supply* law for the Church.

Through custom the Church best accomplishes her end, the salvation of men. Just as the spirit of her penalties is more medicinal than punitive, so also her whole law is less concerned about constraining men within limitations than about leading them firmly but gently towards their final end. It may happen that the universal law, or a particular law, is useless or at least not the best for a certain territory. But an inferior lawmaker can in no way legislate against the law of his superior and in the Church the laity has no legislative power whatsoever. By custom, however, the people can act against the law, and abolish it. This may seem to present a danger, a tendency to relax discipline. Yet, under the conditions to be studied the danger is minimized, while many advantages are still obtainable from custom which *abrogates* law.

The historical synopsis which follows in the first part of this work will show that from the beginning, through the very fact that the Christians obeyed the law, there existed in the Church a phase of custom whereby law was interpreted. From the earliest times also it was known that custom supplied for the deficiency of law.

More slowly and only at a later date was it established in the Church that a custom could even abolish law.

In the second half of this study, which deals with the present law of the Church, it will be demonstrated how the wisdom of the greatest legislator on earth has prudently retained in the new codification customary law, whereby law may be interpreted, supplied and abrogated. An examination will be made of the entire Second Title of the First Book of the Code.

The author wishes to express his gratitude to their Excellencies, the Most Rev. Edward J. Hanna, D.D., and the Most Rev. John J. Mitty, D.D., whose love of clerical scholarship has afforded the opportunity of advanced study.

Deep appreciation is likewise expressed by the writer for the helpful suggestions given him by the Faculty of the School of Canon Law. An appreciative mention of the librarians of the University Library is but small return for the cheerful assistance rendered him at all times.

Part I

THE HISTORICAL DEVELOPMENT OF CUSTOMARY LAW

CHAPTER I

FROM THE BEGINNING OF THE CHURCH TO THE CORPUS JURIS

Article 1. The Fundamental Concept of Custom in the Church

The Founder of the society known as the Catholic Church never wrote a single law. This Founder made it clear that He came not to make void the tradition of the ancients, not to dissolve the law or the prophets. "I came not to dissolve but to fulfill . . . One iota or title shall not pass from the law, till all things be fulfilled."[1]

When Christ had completed that Old Law with His own Testament, He gave no order to His followers to put His law into writing. "Going, therefore teach . . . teaching them to observe all things whatsoever I have commanded you." [2] It was clear from the many words and deeds of the Founder, as well as from the subsequent procedure of His disciples that the new society was to be a living teacher and a legislator.

Whatever enactments have had their origin in the WILL of any such LEGISLATOR *(ex imperio auctoritatis)* make up what may be conveyed by the term LAW *(lex)*. The reaction of the pupil of that living teacher towards the law, the body of usages which has had its origin in the ACTS OF THE PEOPLE, may be called CUSTOM *(consuetudo)*.

Whether either of these is reduced to writing is irrelevant to its nature. Law may be promulgated orally; custom may be written. In the beginning as long as little of the mind of the legislator was consigned to writing, to statute, it was quite natural that custom, the mode of acting by the people at large, should be confused and interwoven with that law which, though unwritten, had its origin

[1] St. Matthew v. 17, 18.

[2] St. Matthew xxviii. 19, 20.

in the will of the legislator. It will be only after centuries that there will appear a clear distinction between the unwritten law of the legislator and the customary law of the people. Practically speaking, however, *consuetudo* soon became known as the unwritten law, *lex,* the written law. To trace the historical growth of customary law in the Church is the burden of the first part of this study.

ARTICLE 2. CUSTOM IN THE FATHERS AND THE EARLY DOCTORS OF THE CHURCH

The unwritten will of the legislator, sometimes called tradition,[3] is mirrored in the acts of the people. It is not surprising, then, to find in the writings of this period no clear-cut distinction between tradition and custom. In the confusion of the two, however, are found vaguely the *notion,* the *import* and the *qualities* of custom during the patristic age.

Early in church history that firebrand Tertullian invokes custom. It is true, reasons Tertullian, that "custom even in civil affairs is taken for law, when law is lacking."[4] But, he argues, a custom must be *reasonable.* "The authority of custom is to be respected, therefore, lest there be no interpreter of reason."[5] And so he concludes that, since it is not reasonable for a soldier to wear a crown, the custom is to be condemned.

Tertullian is bothered about a second practice. Virgins should not go unveiled. Any custom which permits unveiled virgins is erroneous. It opposes *truth,* and "Christ called Himself the truth, not custom. . . . Whatever is against truth is heresy, even if it be ancient custom."[6] Truth for Tertullian means the *jus traditum,* the deposit of faith, written and oral. He, therefore, recognizes the value of custom, provided it be not against reason or against faith.

[3] It is well to note that the word "tradition" is sometimes used to designate juridical tradition or jurisprudence; at times it means the unwritten teaching of Christ transmitted to the faithful by the Church. Tradition, then, is a wider term than custom. It may signify both written and unwritten law; it may embrace both a juridical and a dogmatic content.

[4] Tertullian, *De corona,* c. 4—*MPL,* II, 81.

[5] Tertullian, *De corona,* c. 4—*MPL,* II, 82.

[6] Tertullian, *De virginibus velandis,* c. 1—*MPL,* II, 889.

Epigrammatically he says: *"Traditio tibi praetendetur auctrix, consuetudo confirmatrix et fides observatrix."* [7]

The baptismal controversy in Africa brings out the ideas of Pope St. Stephen and St. Cyprian. The African bishop attempts, it is true, to defend a false doctrine, but what is of interest here is his argument. The custom of not rebaptizing converts from heresy, says St. Cyprian, "must not prevent truth from prevailing. For custom without truth is only error grown old." [8] From Pope St. Stephen came the famous axiom, *"Nil innovetur, nisi quod traditum est."* [9] Here, as all through the patristic age, is noted a natural confusion between tradition and custom.

Turning to the writings of the great Doctors of both the Eastern and the Western Church, there is found the same note of reasonableness and conformity to faith, truth and tradition.

In the East St. Basil writes: "So we must know both what things are of supreme law, and what are customs; we must follow the traditional form in those things which are not stated in the supreme law."[10] And St. Gregory Nazianzen states "Custom holds even in place of law, but all things yield to reason." [11]

In the West the Doctors show the same thought. The great student St. Jerome writes: "I think that you must be admonished that church traditions are to be kept just as they are handed down by the elders (that is, traditions which do not affect the faith) and the custom of one place is not to be subverted by that of others."[12]

After repeating the notions of truth and of reason [13] St. Augustine, that great intellect of the African Church, makes certain clear statements about custom. "In all things concerning which the scriptures state nothing certain, the custom *(mos)* of the people of God

[7] Tertullian, *De corona,* c. 4—*MPL,* II, 80.

[8] S. Cyprian, *Epist. ad Pompeium,* cap. 9—*MPL,* III, 1134. Cyprian's idea is repeated in the Council of Carthage—*MPL,* III, 1064 and 1069.

[9] S. Cyprian, *Epist. LXXIV—MPL,* III, 1010, 1129.

[10] S. Basil, *Epist. CLXXXVIII—MPG,* XXXII, 671.

[11] S. Gregory Naz., *Carminum,* lib. I—*MPG,* XXXVII, 799.

[12] S. Jerome, *Epist. LXXI ad Lucinum—MPL,* XXII, 672.

[13] S. Augustine, *de Baptismo contra Donatistas,* L. IV, c. 5—*MPL,* XLIII, 157; *de Musica,* L. II, cap. VIII & 15—*MPL,* XXXII, 1108; *contra Donatistas,* L. III, c. 6—*MPL,* XLIII, 143.

or the institutions of the elders are *to be kept for law.*"[14] Custom then has force of law but at the same time it is necessary to avoid multiplying practices useless in the Church,[15] and those detracting from piety.[16] So strong is the obligation of custom, thinks Augustine, that just as prevaricators of divine law so also contemners of church customs are to be punished.[17]

St. Gregory the Great adds this statement: "We grant you authority to keep without change every custom which does not prejudice the Catholic faith."[18] Diversity of custom does not harm where there is unity of faith, and if custom "induces hardship on the church, it must be put aside" that the faithful may not be burdened.[19]

The patristic age may be said to end with St. Isidore of Seville in the west and with St. John Damascene in the east. St. Isidore, in his books of the Etymologies has a lexicographical study of the words *lex, jus, mores.* Although his work is not critical, it is not without interest. "The word *jus* is a general term; *lex* is a species of *jus.* All *jus* is composed of *leges* and *mores.*"[20] "Law is written; *mos* is custom approved by age."[21] Isidore's definition reechoes Tertullian, "*Mos* is a long custom, transmitted by usage, and *consuetudo* is a law established by usages, which is taken for law when law is wanting."[22] Time alone will clarify this terminology.

St. John Damascene recalls the fundamental note struck by the founders of the church, that the new society is a living teacher, a legislator independent, if he prefers, of any written law for "the gospel has been promulgated in the whole world without the help of writing."[23] With St. Isidore, then, and with St. John Damascene

[14] S. Augustine, *Epist. XXXVI, Casulano,* c. 1 & 2—*MPL,* XXXIII, 136.

[15] S. Augustine, *Epist. LIV, Januario,* c. 6 & 8—*MPL,* XXXIII, 203.

[16] S. Augustine, *Epist. LV, Januario,* c. 18 & 24—*MPL,* XXXIII, 221.

[17] S. Augustine, *Epist. XXXVI, Casulano,—MPL,* XXXIII, 136.

[18] S. Gregory Great, *Epist. LXXVII,—MPL,* LXXVII, 531.

[19] S. Gregory Great, *Epist. LXVI,—MPL,* LXXVII, 522; *Epist. XLIII,—MPL,* LXXVII, 497.

[20] S. Isidore, *Etymologies,* L. V, c. 3—*MPL,* LXXXII, 199.

[21] S. Isidore, *Etymologies,* L. II, c. 10—*MPL,* LXXXII, 130.

[22] S. Isidore, *Etymologies,* L. II, c. 10—*MPL,* LXXXII, 130; L. V, c. 3—*MPL,* LXXXII, 199.

[23] S. John Damascene, *De imaginibus,* oratio 11—*MPG,* XCIV, 1303.

the patristic period closes. The collection of Gratian will repeat the teaching of many of the Fathers, and will bridge his period with this era. It has been noted that during this time there is no clear distinction between tradition, which comes from the will of the legislator, and custom, which arises in the will of the people. For the Fathers tradition and custom are but two sides of the same shield.

CHAPTER II

CUSTOM IN THE CORPUS JURIS CIVILIS—JUSTINIAN LAW

Article 1. The Notion of Custom, Its Terminology

The notion of custom, as it developed in Roman Law, influenced Canon Law down to the end of the middle ages. It is of importance, therefore, to study something of customary law found in the legislation of Justinian, before proceeding to an investigation of the *Corpus Juris Canonici.*

The Roman Law "is composed either of written or of non-written law." [1] This division, however, into written and non-written law is merely a verbal dichotomy. Writing is not of the essence of custom; it is already a law, *jus non scriptum,* and its legal force in no way depends on writing. But there is nothing to prevent it from being put into script. In like manner *lex,* or the *jus scriptum,* can be promulgated orally. This division is of no practical value in Justinian and seems to have originated simply from Greek antithesis ἄγραφοι ἔγγραφοι. [2]

Many words are found in the Corpus, which indicate the unwritten law, or custom. It is called *usus, mos, mores, mores maiorum, antiquitas, observantia, vetustas, consuetudo usu comprobata.* The word *consuetudo* alone, which was destined to designate what is known today as custom, is not found frequently in the sources. And when that word is used, it generally does not imply a legal obligation.[3] Indeed the habit of doves in returning to their dovecote, the manner in which the vinedresser prunes his vines, married life, are all connoted in various ways by *consuetudo.*[4] The somewhat strange plural use of the word "customs" in English originates from the

[1] *Ins.* (1, 2) 3; *Ins.* (1, 2) 10.

[2] E. C. Clark, *Roman Private Law,* Cambridge, 1914, I, 313.

[3] D. (28, 1) 21. 1; D. (32, 75); D. (34, 2) 32. 2; D. (5, 3) 54.2.

[4] D. (10, 2) 8. 1; D. (5, 3) 54. 2; *Ins.* (1, 9) 1.

time when Justinian called the tax revenues, ***consuetudines***.[5] In general it may be said that the word ***consuetudo*** implies legal obligation only when it is in juxtaposition to ***jus scriptum***. This will be noted in texts throughout this study.

Justinian gives no definition of custom. But without attempting to make a composite definition from many citations, the best definition perhaps is found in these words.

> Ex non scripto ius venit, quod usus comprobavit. Nam diuturni mores consensu utentium comprobati legem imitantur.[6]

This is the law which Cicero spoke of long before Justinian,—a law "quod voluntate omnium sine lege vetustas comprobavit." [7]

Article 2. The Essence of Custom—The Efficient Cause

In Roman Law the efficient cause of custom is the people.

> Inveterata consuetudo pro lege non immerito custoditur, et hoc est jus quod dicitur moribus constitutum. Nam cum ipsae leges nulla alia ex causa nos teneant, quam quod iudicio populi receptae sunt, merito et ea, quae sine ullo scripto populus probavit, tenebunt omnes: nam quid interest suffragio populus voluntatem suam declaret an ipsis rebus et factis? [8]

It has been said that this passage is "full of errors." It is objected that the custom spoken of is provincial. But granted that the citation refers to a particular situation, the principles are general. "The reasoning refers to the Roman legislature when the Populus was still perhaps in theory sovereign (having been so in reality at the earlier time, which Julian doubtless had in mind)." [9] It would seem, then, that an objection on the ground that the government in the time of Hadrian was a monarchy does not devaluate the doctrine contained

[5] N. 8; N. 30; N. 73; N. 128; C. (1, 2) 24. 12; C. (1, 27) 2. 35. *Cf.* Wehrle, *De La Coutume*, p. 13.

[6] *Ins.* (1, 2) 9.

[7] Cicero, *de inv.*, 2, 22, 67.

[8] D. (1, 3) 32; *Ins.* (3, 10) pr.

[9] E. C. Clark, *Roman Private Law*, Cambridge, 1914, I, 346.

in these words. The people are the efficient cause, are themselves the legislator in custom. So Justinian maintains the above text even in his age, when full government had passed into the hands of the Emperor, and he explains:

> Quod principi placuit, legis habet vigorem: utpote cum lege regia, quae de imperio eius lata est, populus ei et in eum omne suum imperium et potestatem conferat.[10]

The people then are the efficient cause of custom. In statute law the legislator shows his will explicitly; in customary law the people speak tacitly:

> Sed et ea, quae longa consuetudine comprobata sunt ac per annos plurimos observata, velut tacita civium conventio non minus quam ea quae scripta sunt iura servantur.[11]

Thus all the usages, the practices and even the responses of jurisprudence are only manifestations of the will of the people. In a word "from the non-written law comes a law which use has approved. For ancient practices approved by the consent of the users imitates law."[12]

Article 3. Legal Requisites of Acts in Custom

Acts show the will of a people, which is the source of custom. But not every act, as is evident, correctly shows the will of the citizens. Custom must have certain qualities.

[10] D. (1, 4) 1.

The emperor Hadrian (117-138) put an end to the Praetorian edict and claimed the power of direct legislation for himself. This usurpation was cloaked over by the *lex regia*. This was a fiction, whereby the people were supposed to have conferred sovereignty on the emperor. This theoretical basis was solidified so that the emperor in time became sole legislator.

Perhaps the first attempt at codification was the XII Tables (451-448 B. C.). Certain it is that unwritten laws remained outside the Code. Justinian attempted to embrace the *lex* in his Code and the *jus* in his Digest. But unwritten law or custom still existed outside the legislation written by Justinian.

[11] D. (1, 3) 35. *Civitas, regio, locus, provincia* are named as subjects of custom in C. (4, 65) 8; D. (18, 1) 71; D. (1, 3) 34; D. (18, 1) 34. 1.

[12] *Ins.* (1, 2) 9; *Ins.* (1, 2) 11.

A. Reasonableness

Reasonableness is a definite quality of custom, as it must be of all law. A custom may be viewed in respect to the public utility, or in respect to the written law. If a custom must be reasonable in regard to the written law, this would mean that a custom could never be against the law. This question of *ratio juris,* of custom versus the law, is treated in a following number. In regard to the public good custom certainly must be reasonable. For the Romans every custom, since it proceeded from the will of the people, was reasonable (*ratione utilitatis*). Several citations have been offered to show that Roman Law demands reasonableness.[13]

> nam ea consuetudo praecedens et ratio quae consuetudinem suasit custodienda est, et ne quid contra longam consuetudinem fiat, ad sollicitudinem suam revocabit praeses provinciae. Consuetudo . . . non . . . rationem vincat.[14]

It must be admitted that the meaning of *ratio* in these texts is not clear.[15] The note of reasonableness (*ratio juris*), as it will be found later in Canon Law, is not discovered in the sources of Justinian Law. The distinction of custom, good and bad, approved and disapproved, as understood by canonists, does not find place among the civilists. All customs are reasonable, because they begin with the people, the source of law.

B. The Time Element

Another positive quality of custom is time. Many temporal expressions are found in Justinian Law. Custom is modified by such adjectives as *longa, inveterata, diuturna, mores maiorum, usus longaevus, comprobata, antiquitus probata, per annos plurimos observata.*[16] Many are the expressions of time, but nowhere does Justinian speak of a limited, definite, set time.[17] There does not appear

[13] C. (8, 52) 1.

[14] C. (8, 52) 2. *Cf.* N. 134, c. 1 in fine; C. (1, 3) 38.2.

[15] D'Angelo, *Jus digestorum,* I, n. 122.

[16] D. (1, 3) 35; D. (1, 3) 32; C. (8, 52) 2; C. (8, 52) 1.3; D. (1, 3) 33.

[17] *Ins.* (2, 6) pr. This text speaks of prescription and long time possession. "*Res immobiles*" are prescribed by long time. Long time is considered 10 years for those present, 20 for the absent. *Cf.* also N. 106.

in the law of Justinian any indication that custom depends on prescribed time. Time differs with each custom, which the magistrate or prince judges.[18]

C. *Error in Custom*

If the people are in error concerning the law, has their custom, so introduced, any influence on the law? One text concerning this matter has been variously interpreted.

> Quod non ratione introductum, sed errore primum, deinde consuetudine optentum est, in aliis similibus non optinet.[19]

Whether this text stresses "*ratione*" or "*errore*" has long been argued. Nor is it clear whether "*similia*" refers to later cases or merely to analogous application.[20] Some have concluded that the Romanists held an erroneous custom valid but not liable to analogous extension.[21] Probably, however, it should be concluded with Biondi that custom cannot originate in error, since the people must intend to produce custom.[22]

D. *The Intention*

The acts which introduce custom should be performed with a legal conviction, that is, with the intention of binding oneself to a law. The mere performance of actions would constitute only observance. To produce a legal obligation the practice must have a legal character, namely the binding force of law, in the mind of the person performing the acts.[23] The notion of intention is not found in the texts of the sources. However, it would have been a very easy deduction, because for the Romanists the people were the efficient cause of custom.

E. *Qualities Implied*

That the acts performed must be general, frequent, uniform and uninterrupted are characteristics which cannot be found clearly in

18 Cicognani, *Jus. can.*, II, 164, 165; C. (1, 14) 11.
19 D. (1, 3) 39.
20 Brie, *Gewohnheitsrecht*, I, 27, 28.
21 Van Hove, *De consuet.*, n. 132; *cf.* D. (1, 3) 14.
22 Biondi, *Corso di Istituzioni*, p. 35.
23 Biondi, *Corso di Istituzioni*, p. 35.

the sources. They are rather logical conclusions from the principles of customary law. This study will be developed by canonists.

Article 4. The Juridical Value of Custom

A custom may be in harmony with the law, over and above the law, or against the law; it may therefore interpret, supply or abolish law. Each kind will be treated respectively.

A. Custom Conformed to Law

There is a text which was destined to find a celebrated place verbatim in the codification of Canon Law.

> Si de interpretatione legis quaeratur, in primis inspiciendum est quo iure civitas retro in eiusmodi casibus usa fuisset; optima enim est legum interpres consuetudo.[24]

There is another text which must be studied parallel to the preceding.

> in ambiguitatibus quae ex legibus proficiscuntur consuetudinem aut rerum perpetuo similiter iudicatarum auctoritatem vim legis optinere debere.[25]

The principle enunciated in the first text that custom is the best interpreter of laws may be understood to refer to a practice which existed, *before* the law was enacted. When legislation is about to be made then it is best interpreted by the practice of the people, and prudence dictates that it be framed with a view to the spontaneous actions of the people. Hence the axiom that custom is the best interpreter of laws *to be made*.[26] The axiom has come to be applied, however, rather to the interpretation of laws already made.

The second text, a rescript of Severus, which also speaks of the interpretation of law, refers rather to doubtful laws, *in ambiguitatibus*.

Both texts, therefore, deal with the interpretation of laws by custom. The distinction between the two texts was not noted by the

[24] D. (1, 3) 37; Code of Canon Law, Canon 29.

[25] D. (1, 3) 38.

[26] Flumene, *La consuetudine*, p. 215.

commentators of Roman Law. Suarez will later explain the difference between practice which interprets a clear law and custom which interprets a doubtful law. He will introduce the distinction between a doctrinal and an authentic interpretation.[27]

B. Custom Beside the Law

The second effect of custom is to fill in the lacunae in the law, to supply when law is lacking. In early times indeed custom was almost the sole font of law. Many fundamental institutes, such as *dominium, patria potestas,* originated in custom. Even the *leges regiae* and the *jus Papirianum* are ancient customs which past generations wished to call laws.[28] The sources show ample evidence of this juridical value, the supplying of law by custom when the written law is silent.[29]

C. Custom Against the Law

The conflict between the statute and a custom presents a great problem in the study of customary law. Can there really be a custom with power to abolish law? In the sources there is evidence for both an affirmative and a negative answer.

(a) Affirmative

It seems difficult to explain away the force of certain texts, which speak of custom abolishing law.

[27] Giacchi, *Della Interpretazione,* Milano, 1935, p. 39; Suarez, *de leg.,* L. VII, c. 17, n. 2, *cf. infra* 51.

[28] Biondi, *Istituzioni,* p. 34.

[29] Sed et ea, quae longa consuetudine comprobata sunt ac per annos plurimos observata, velut tacita civium conventio non minus quam ea quae scripta sunt servantur.—D. (1, 3) 35.

De quibus causis scriptis legibus non utimur, id custodiri oportet quod moribus et consuetudine inductum est.—D. (1, 3) 32 prin.

Diuturna consuetudo pro iure et lege in his quae non ex scripto descendunt observari solet.—D. (1, 3) 33.

Leges quoque ipsas antiquitus probata et servata tenaciter consuetudo imitatur et retinet: et quod officiis curiis civitatibus principiis vel collegiis praestitum fuisse cognoscitur, perpetuae legis vicem obtinere statuimus.—C. (8, 52) 3.

> nam cum ipsae leges nulla alia ex causa nos teneat, quam quod iudicio populi receptae sunt, merito et ea, quae sine ullo scripto populus probavit, tenebunt omnes: nam quid interest suffragio populus voluntatem suam declaret an rebus ipsis et factis? Quare rectissime etiam illud receptum est, ut leges non solum suffragio legislatoris sed etiam tacito consensu omnium per desuetudinem abrogentur.[30]
> Quae ipsa sibi quaeque civitas constituit, saepe mutari solent vel tacito consensu populi vel alia postea lege lata.[31]
> . . . in multis capitulis lex Papia ab anterioribus principibus emendata fuit et per desuetudinem abolita.[32]
> Licet a Constantino . . . in constitutione . . . quaedam . . . , haec non respicimus, quoniam et non utendo perempta est.[33]

It seems necessary, therefore, to yield to these texts and admit that custom can abolish law.

(b) Negative

Of all the texts in the sources pertinent to this question, perhaps the most celebrated is that of Constantine, which was destined to find its way verbatim into the Decretals of Gregory IX.

> Consuetudinis ususque longaevi non vilis auctoritas est, verum non usque adeo sui valitura momento, ut aut rationem vincat aut legem.[34]

This doctrine, it seems, clearly forbids custom against the law. In the conflict of these contradicting texts can truth be found? Does Roman Law admit a custom with power to abrogate the written law?

(c) Conclusion

There are not lacking writers who claim that a choice is impossible. They are content to observe that the texts are contradictory. The statement of Constantine clearly forbids customs against the

[30] D. (1, 3) 32. *Cf.* Pernice, *Zum römischen Gewohnheitsrechte,* Z. S. S., XX, pp. 156-162.

[31] *Ins.* (1, 2) 11.

[32] C. (6, 51) 1. 1.

[33] C. (6, 51) 1.1.

[34] C. (8, 52) 2; D. (22, 1) 1; N. (106, 1); c. 11, X, *de consuetudine,* I, 4.

law; the Digest evidently upholds such customs.[35] Others, however, have made various attempts to effect a reconcilation. (a) Some would say that Constantine merely affirms that custom has no greater force than law, but he does not deny it equal force. In other words, custom is not so great that a consequent law cannot derogate it, even without express mention. Custom on the other hand may abolish law with the legal consent of the ruler.[36] (b) Others find an interpretation by understanding that the lawmaker has in mind a particular custom which is in conflict with a general law, expressly abrogating customs.[37] (c) Still others, following the historical school of Scialoia think that the word *"lex"* means a law which abrogates custom and the word *"ratio"* signifies the social order. Constantine, therefore, says simply that custom cannot override a law with an abrogating clause or upset the whole juridical order.[38] (d) The foregoing explanations of the law of Constantine all assume that the customs of which the emperor speaks are the ordinary customs which might originate within the empire. But the truest doctrine seems to be that of Biondi. He finds a simple answer in the historical setting of the texts which appear contradictory. During the post-classical era there came into existence a customary law outside the Roman legal system. This was accentuated by the edict of Caracalla, which gave citizenship to all inhabitants of the empire. It was natural, therefore, that a conflict should arise between the law of the empire and the various national usages, which flourished in the provinces. It is these practices of the provinces then to which Constantine directed his constitution.[39]

It seems possible, then, to reconcile the text of Constantine, which appears to deny custom against the law, with those several text which clearly admit such custom. From the Justinian Law, from the letter of the texts, it should be concluded that custom against the law is tolerated. The text of Constantine will insinuate itself into the study of Canon Law. The words of the emperor will be taken over by

[35] Pacchioni, *Di Diritto Romano,* p. 353.

[36] Cicognani, *Jus can.,* II, 153; Ferrini, *Pandette,* n. 17; Toso, *Comment. min.,* I, 76, note 1.

[37] Mitteis, *Reichsrecht,* p. 163, n. 2.

[38] Bonfante, *Istituzioni,* art. 7, p. 24; D'Angelo, *Jus Digestorum,* I, 85.

[39] Biondi, *Istituzioni,* p. 36.

Pope Gregory IX and with a certain suffix they will be used by that Pontiff, when he legislates concerning custom against ecclesiastical law.

Article 5. The Proof of Custom

In the early days of juridical development there is no need of proving a custom. It is considered an evident source of law.

> immo magnae auctoritatis hoc ius habetur, quod in tantum probatum est, ut non fuerit necesse scripto id comprehendere.[40]

At this time, then, it is the duty of the judge to invoke the custom. As a savant of all law he is expected to know both the statute and the customary law.

> Illud observare debet judex, ne aliter iudicet quam legibus aut constitutionibus aut moribus proditum est.[41]

Soon, however, the statute law begins to replace the customary law. Custom then is presumed merely a fact until it has been proved by the parties that it has qualified to become a law. The clearest and most definite proof which the parties can give is to cite a judgment wherein a decision has been given in favor of that custom, to quote precedent.[42]

When the parties cannot find a previous court sentence to prove a custom, they must begin the usual court procedure through witnesses. Justinian does not outline the method of proof. Some indication however may be found in the case treated by Novel CVI.[43]

Custom then plays no small part in the law of the *Corpus Juris Civilis*. During the age of the Decretists and Decretalists it was fused, as an alloy, into the canonical system. But first there must follow a chapter on the *Corpus Juris Canonici* itself.

[40] D. (1, 3) 36.

[41] *Ins.* (4, 17) pro.; D. (22, 5) 3.6; C. (2, 10) 1.

[42] Cum de consuetudine civitatis vel provinciae confidere quis videtur, primum quidem illud explorandum arbitror, an etiam contradicto aliquando iudicio consuetudo firmata est. D. (1, 3) 34.

Praeses provinciae probatis his, quae in oppido frequenter in eodem genere controversiarum servata sunt, causa cognita statuet. C. (8, 52) 1.

[43] *Cf.* Wehrle, *De La Coutume*, p. 24.

CHAPTER III

CUSTOM IN THE CORPUS JURIS CANONICI

Article 1. The Decree of Gratian

About the year 1150 the great jurist Gratian made his famous compilation. Concerning custom he presents little or nothing new since the patristic age. But Gratian summarizes well the teaching of the past. His very many texts about custom, since they are gathered from his predecessors, bridge his age with the patristic era. He shows that custom has an extensive scope and out of many citations can be formed the nucleus of a doctrine soon to be developed.

1. Notion of Custom

The notion of custom is fully understood only when all its elements are developed. Gratian's notion, therefore, is not a precise definition.

> Cum itaque dicitur: "non differt utrum consuetudo scriptura vel ratione consistat," apparet quod consuetudo partim est redacta in scriptis, partim moribus tantum utentium est reservata. Quae in scriptis redacta est, constitutio sive jus vocatur; quod vero in scriptis redacta non est, generali nomine, consuetudo videlicet appellatur.[1]

It is noted that custom is the product of an ecclesiastical community. It is not the act of an individual.[2] No communities are indicated specifically, but the *Decretum* speaks of customs of the *ecclesiae, pro loco, ecclesiae romanae, universae ecclesiae.*[3]

2. Some Qualities of Custom

The qualities needed by custom are the same required in the past. Its fundamental note is reason.[4] Customs not reasonable are

[1] *Dictum Gratiani post* c. 5, D. 1.

[2] C. 8, D. 100; c. 3, D. 11.

[3] C. 8, D. 100; c. 3, D. 12; c. 12, D. 12; c. 11, D. 11; c. 10, D. 12.

[4] C. 5, D. I; c. 7, D. XII; c. 4, D. VIII; c. 5, D. VIII; c. 7, D. VIII.

pravus usus, mala consuetudo, corruptela.[5] Its second adjective is truth. Truth embraces the natural law.

> Quaecumque enim vel moribus recepta sunt . . . si naturali juri fuerint adversa, vana et irrita sunt habenda . . . Liquido igitur apparet quod consuetudo naturali juri postponitur.[6]

A third notion of longevity is indicated; custom must attain a certain age.[7]

3. Kinds of Custom

A custom may be in harmony with the written law, contrary to it, or over and above it. This division which gives a threefold value or effect of custom begins to be outlined in the collection of Gratian. A custom may be in harmony with law or conformed to law. "Leges . . . firmantur, cum moribus utentium approbantur." [8] A custom may be over and above the law, that is, beside the law. Gratian cites many of the Fathers on this point. In a word his doctrine is that long usages institute law, and a law . . . "quod pro lege suscipitur cum deficit lex." [9] Yet he would not have particular customs multiplied.[10] Finally a custom may be contrary or against the law. Does Gratian hold for the validity of such a custom? A juxtaposition of texts leaves the question somewhat obscure, although a conclusion may be drawn.

(a) Certain words would seem to indicate that the author of the Decree does not admit that a custom can supersede the law. Gratian quotes the celebrated text of Constantine.

> Consuetudinis ususque longaevi non vilis auctoritas est. Verum non usque adeo sui valitura momento ut aut rationem vincat aut legem scriptam.[11]

Although the meaning of Constantine has been disputed,[12] the inter-

[5] C. 1, D. XI; c. 3, D. VIII.

[6] *Dictum Gratiani post* c. 1, D. VIII; *dictum Gratiani post* c. 9, D. VIII.

[7] C. 4, D. I; c. 6, D. XII; c. 7, D. XII.

[8] *Dictum Gratiani post* c. 3, D. IV.

[9] C. 5, D. I; c. 7, D. XI; c. 8, D. XII; c. 3, D. XII; c. 7, D. XII.

[10] *Dictum Gratiani post* c. 11, D. XII.

[11] C. 4, D. XI; C. (8, 52) 2.

[12] *Cf. supra* 15.

pretation taken by Gratian seems clear from his words which he adds to the *dictum,*

> Cum vero nec sacris canonibus nec humanis legibus consuetudo obviare monstratur, inconcussa servanda est.[13]

A second text from Roman Law is found in Gratian. *Diuturni mores consensu utentium approbati legem imitantur.*[14] After the word *"mores,"* the text of the *Decretum* has added to the words of the Institutes, *"nisi legi sunt adversi."*[15] These two texts, then, would lead one to think that the author of the *Decretum* does not admit a custom against the law, that ". . . *legibus consuetudo cedat."* Other texts substantiate this opinion.[16]

(b) There is not lacking evidence on the other hand that tends to move the pendulum in favor of custom against the law.

> Unde illud Telesphori Papae . . . quia moribus utentium approbatum non est, aliter agentes, transgressionis reos non arguit.[17]

This reasoning rests on an old principle of Roman Law, which became fundamental during the Middle Ages, namely, that acceptance confirms a law. And this is what Gratian says in the words immediately preceding the above text,

> Leges instituuntur, cum promulgantur, firmantur, cum moribus utentium approbantur. Sicut enim moribus utentium in contrarium nonnullae leges hodie abrogatae sunt, ita moribus utentium ipsae leges confirmantur.[18]

(c) Conclusion concerning custom against the law.

A reconciliation of the texts of Gratian might be effected through the following distinctions:

1. A law is confirmed by acceptance on the part of the people.

[13] *Dictum Gratiani post* c. 4, D. XI.

[14] *Ins.* (1, 2) 9.

[15] C. 6, D. XII.

[16] *Dictum Gratiani* in D. XI; c. 3, D. XII; c. 1, D. XI; c. 2, D. XI; c. 3, D. VIII.

[17] *Dictum Gratiani post* c. 3, D. IV.

[18] *Dictum Gratiani post* c. 3, D. IV.

2. A law not yet received in use is a law unconfirmed.
3. There cannot be a custom against a law already received in use.
4. Perhaps, there may be a custom against a law not yet received.

The first two conclusions can be made because at this period the relation between the legislator and the people in the formation of customary law had not yet been clearly studied. Only later will it be affirmed that the constitutional and legislative power of the Church is in no way, even in custom, subservient to the people's will to accept or to reject a law.

The third inference is drawn because the text cited in favor of a contrary custom does not refer to the abrogation of a *law already flourishing* but only to the acceptance or non-acceptance of a *law just passed.*[19]

The fourth conclusion contains the qualified statement "perhaps," for this reason. When Gratian has said, "Those who act against this statute are not guilty of transgression, because it was not approved by the practice of the users," he seems to sustain the conclusion that there can be a custom against a law not yet received. But speaking of the same text in another chapter Gratian uses a tantalizing, qualifying clause, *"nisi forte quis dicat haec non decernendo esse statuta, sed exhortando conscripta."* [20] And, therefore, it may be concluded that Gratian generally does not favor a custom against established law.

Article 2. The Decretals of Gregory IX

By the Bull *Rex pacificus* issued in 1234 Pope Gregory IX promulgated his Decretals as the first authentic collection of ecclesiastical law. In it he gives the first official doctrine on custom. Out of different terminology the word *consuetudo* comes into most frequent use. Pope Gregory no longer confounds tradition and custom, as his predecessors had done. His definition of custom, however, is not

[19] Brie, *Die Lehre vom Gewohnheitsrecht,* p. 79—followed by Michiels, *Normae Generales,* II, 18, and Van Hove, *De consuet.,* n. 29, against Bauduin, *De consuet.,* n. 63; Phillips, *Kirchenrecht,* III, 726, and Wernz, *Jus Decretalium,* I, n. 187, III,—who think Gratian means a particular custom cannot abolish a general law; only a general custom can do so.

[20] *Dictum Gratiani post* c. 6, D. IV.

original. He retains Gratian's idea, which in turn was derived from Justinian and St. Isidore.

> Consuetudo autem est ius moribus institutum . . . Vocatur consuetudo, quia in communi est usu.[21]

Customs are the product of a community, not of a single person.[22] Some of the communities capable of introducing custom are indicated implicitly when the Decretals mention custom of *ecclesiae, civitatis, ecclesiae metropolitanae, provinciae, dioecesis, archidioecesis municipii, alicujus terrae, regni, quorumdam locorum, regionis, ecclesiae Romanae.*[23]

There seems to be no direct statement in the Decretals themselves concerning the consent of a legislator to custom.[24]

The threefold juridical character of custom becomes more evident in the Decretals. A custom may be *conformed* to law and indeed the rule is enunciated that *"consuetudo est optima legum interpres."*[25] As the earliest writers had already done so too Gregory IX offers countless examples of custom beside the law.[26] These customs beside the law have some authority and should not be set aside by every wind and whim of thought.[27] The most celebrated chapter on cus-

[21] C. 5, D. I; *Ins.* (1, 2) 9; S. Isidore, *Etymologies,* L. II, c. 10—*MPL,* LXXXII, 131.

[22] C. 2, X, *de consuetudine,* I, 4; c. 10, X, *de testamentis et ultimis voluntatibus,* III, 26.

[23] C. 13, X, *de celebratione missarum, et sacramento eucharistiae et divinis officiis,* III, 41; c. 2, 3, X, *de observatione ieiuniorum,* III, 46; c. 7, X, *de consuetudine,* I, 4; c. 7, 9, X, *de sepulturis,* III, 28; c. 26, X, *de testibus et attestationibus,* II, 20; c. 16, X, *de praescriptionibus,* II, 26; c. 8, X, *de sententia et re iudicata,* II, 27; c. 8, X, *de in integrum restitutione,* I, 41; c. 5, X, *de auctoritate et usu pallii,* I, 8; c. 50, X, *de electione et electi potestate,* I, 6; c. 3, X, *de causa possessionis et proprietatis,* II, 12; c. 11, X, *de regulis juris,* V, 41.

[24] C. 8, X, *de consuetudine,* I, 4; c. 4, X, *de postulatione praelatorum,* I, 5, treat rather of the consent of the community.—*Cf.* Van Hove, *De consuet.,* p. 49, note 3.

[25] C. 1, X, *de consuetudine,* I, 4; c. 8, X, *de consuetudine,* I, 4.

[26] C. 6, X, *de his, quae fiunt a praelato sine consensu capituli,* III, 10; c. 7, X, *de appellationibus, recusationibus, et relationibus,* II, 28; c. 13, X, *de judiciis,* II, 1; c. 5, X, *de foro competenti,* II, 2; c. 9, X, *de fide instrumentorum,* II, 22.

[27] C. 9, *de consuetudine,* I, 4.

tomary law antedating the codification of Canon Law is the following which speaks of custom ***against the law.***

> Quum tanto sint graviora peccata, quanto diutius infelicem animam detinent alligatam, nemo sanae mentis intelligit, naturali juri, cujus transgressio periculum salutis inducit, quacumque consuetudine, quae dicenda est verius in hac parte corruptela, posse aliquatenus derogari. Licet etiam longaevae consuetudinis non sit vilis auctoritas, non tamen est usque adeo valitura, ut vel juri positivo debeat praejudicium generare, nisi fuerit rationabilis et legitime sit praescripta.[28]

Before analyzing the decretal *Quum Tanto* of Gregory IX, it will be well to note here the teaching of earlier Pontiffs concerning a custom against the law. These Decretals Gregory has collected. They will show the transition between Gratian and Gregory in this all important question of custom opposed to law. Gratian wrote about the year 1150. Not long after Pope Alexander III expressed agreement with the *Decretum*

> sicut consuetudo laudabilis nulla debet novitate convelli, sic quod noscitur contra jus moribus introductum obvia ratione debet dissolvi.[29]

And again the same Pope says:

> licet usus vel consuetudinis non minima sit auctoritas, numquam tamen veritati aut legi praejudicat.[30]

Lucius III, the successor of Alexander adopted the same view as Gratian,

> . . . consuetudine, quae est legi contraria, non obstante, iuramentum calumniae subire cogatur.[31]

So too Clement III and Honorius III seem to reject custom against the law. The texts, however, might refer to a simple reprobation of

[28] C. 11, X, *de consuetudine,* I, 4.

[29] C. 2, X, *de probationibus,* II, 19; c. 4, X, *de officio archidiaconi,* I, 23.

[30] C. 8, X, *de sententia et re judicata,* II, 27; c. 8, X, *de simonia, et ne aliquid pro spiritualibus exigatur vel promittatur,* V, 3.

[31] C. 3, X, *de fideiussoribus,* III, 22; c. 8, *de iudiciis,* II, 1.

particular customs.[32] A transition is seen in the pontificate of Innocent III, who anticipated Gregory IX by admitting custom against the law . . . talis fuerit consuetudo probata, quae iuri communi praeiudicet.[33] An examination of the chapter of Gregory IX will reveal that the legislator demands of custom four qualities, two of which are negative and two positive.

1. Custom must not prejudice natural law. This is an evident quality, demanded by all canonists. For Gregory, however, the natural law implies a wide scope, embracing not only the divine positive law of the two Testaments, but also the principles of natural reason.

2. Custom must not prejudice positive Church law. Even long custom cannot prejudice positive law, says Gregory. He will qualify this statement presently. Custom cannot be against the sacred canons or the Church's liberty, in a word, the welfare of the faith. Long is the list of customs in the Decretals which are called null by positive law. Such customs are condemned and are tagged with adjectives like "pernicious," "disgraceful," "detestable," "reprehensible," "enemy of discipline," "corruptible." [34] From all these citations and from the first words of the chapter *Quum Tanto,* it seems that Gregory IX rejects a custom against the law. But he ends the sentence with the qualification "unless it be reasonable and legitimately prescribed."

3. Custom must be reasonable. This is an old quality demanded by the earliest writers. But in the Decretals reasonableness means much more than not contrary to the natural law or the deposit of faith. A custom may be in harmony with the natural law and yet be unreasonable, because it is against certain ecclesiastical law. When cus-

[32] C. 26, X, *de testibus et attestationibus,* II, 20; c. 10, X, *de consuetudine,* I. 4.

[33] C. 8, X, *de consuetudine,* I, 4; c. 13, X, *de iudiciis,* II, 1; c. 3, X, *de causa possessionis et proprietatis,* II, 12; c. 29, X, *de verborum significatione,* V, 40.

[34] C. 13, X, *de sepulturis,* III, 28; c. 4, X, *de cohabitatione clericorum et mulierum,* III, 2; c. 26, X, *de appellationibus, recusationibus, et relationibus,* II, 28; c. 5, X, *de consuetudine,* I, 4; c. 56, X, *de electione et electi potestate,* I, 6.

tom is opposed to canonical institutions, it should have no effect and judicial sentence should be given after the case has been drawn up as the order of reason demands.[35] The judgment of the reasonableness of a custom in respect to the law depends upon the legislator. Some he may call "good," "approved," "laudable."[36] Others are designated as "corruptions," "abuse," "not reasonable."[37] It is clear that the Decretals give a wider scope to the meaning of the term "reasonableness."[38] Some of the reprobations found in the Decretals are couched in these phrases: *talem consuetudinem reprobamus,... irritamus, eo quod minus rationabilis habeatur, talem consuetudinem declaramus irritam.*[39] These and other similar clauses are used in reprobating certain customs which may not in themselves be unreasonable.

4. Custom must be legitimately prescribed. This final quality is something new, a development of Gregory IX. Before the time of Gregory there were such expressions as "longevity," "immemorial custom," "prescription," "law or custom already prescribed," "custom pacifically introduced," "custom approved."[40] Such were the expressions used up to the time of Gregory. But he it is who coins

[35] C. 3, X, *de consuetudine,* I, 4; c. 1, X, *de his, quae fiunt a maiori parte capituli,* III, 11.

[36] C. 3, X, *de eo, qui mittitur in possessione causa rei servandae,* II, 15; c. 8, X, *de consuetudine,* I, 4; c. 31, X, *de electione et electi potestate,* I, 6; c. 2, X, *de probationibus,* II, 19; c. 42, X, *de simonia, et ne aliquid pro spiritualibus exigatur vel promittatur,* V, 3; c. 13, X, *de sepulturis,* III, 28; c. 2, X, *de consuetudine,* I, 4.

[37] C. 6, X, *de iure patronatus,* III, 38; c. 14, X, *de electione et electi potestate,* I, 6; c. 3, X, *de magistris, et ne aliquid exigatur pro licentia docendi,* V, 5; c. 5, 7, 10, 11, X, *de consuetudine,* I, 4; c. 13, X, *de celebratione missarum, et sacramento eucharistiae et divinis officiis,* III, 41; c. 2, X, *de clericis pugnantibus in duello,* V. 14.

[38] C. 4, X, *de consuetudine,* I, 4; c. 13, X, *de officio iudicis ordinarii,* I, 31; c. 8, X, *de simonia, et ne aliquid pro spiritualibus exigatur vel promittatur,* V, 3; c. 20, X, *de praescriptionibus,* II, 26; c. 9, X, *de sepulturis,* III, 28; c. 13, X, *de celebratione missarum, et sacramento eucharistiae et divinis officiis,* III, 41.

[39] C. 3, 5, 10, X, *de consuetudine,* I, 4; c. 4, X, *de probationibus,* II, 19.

[40] C. 13, X, *de sententia et re judicata,* II, 27; c. 26, X, *de verborum significatione,* V, 40; c. 17, X, *de praescriptionibus,* II, 26; c. 4, X, *de electione et electi potestate,* I, 6; c. 10, X, *de officio archidiaconi,* I, 23.

an expression still in circulation, *consuetudo legitime praescripta.*[41] What does Gregory mean? Why does he choose this expression?

If Gregory speaks of true prescription, then all the qualities of prescription must be present:

> Non usucapies, nisi sint tibi talia quinque: Sit res apta, fides, titulus, possessio, tempus.

A comprehensive study of the chapter, however, shows that the Pontiff does not mean real prescription. The whole chapter clearly treats of a norm for action.

Although Gregory does not refer to real prescription, yet the very notion of a temporal element in custom originated in prescription. For a time custom was considered by some as a prescription against the law. Soon it became manifest that there is a clear line of demarcation between prescription and custom. Although it was established that custom was not prescription, it was likewise agreed that through prescription there could be acquired privileges. Such privileges acquired by prescription against the common law were called customs, *consuetudines,* because as a matter of fact they were obtained through the repeated acts of many persons, namely a corporation. So through the concepts of prescription and privilege, the notion of time in custom developed.[42]

Thus the concept of custom in the Decretals is distinct from that of prescription and privilege, even though the element of time in customary law grew out of the two latter notions. But why does Gregory coin the indefinite expression, "custom legitimately and canonically prescribed"? Does this expression carry the note of definite or indefinite time? It seems clear that all customs against the general law, whether they were particular or universal, had to run a definite time.[43] The chapter *Quum Tanta* also regulates customs against particular laws for the broad terminology "*juri*

[41] C. 11, X, *de consuetudine,* I, 4; c. 50, X, *de electione et electi potestate,* I, 6; c. 3, X, *de causa possessionis et proprietatis,* II, 12.

[42] Köstler, "Consuetudo legitime praescripta," *Zeitschrift d. Savigny-Stift.,* Kan. Abt. XXXIX (1918) 154-194.

[43] C. 11, X, *de consuetudine,* I, 4; c. 3, X, *de causa possessionis et proprietatis,* II, 12.

positivo" includes all kinds of law. It seems to have been with some deliberation that Gregory picked his phraseology. Perhaps he wished to pilot a wide course between the disputed alternatives of ten, forty and one hundred years' duration. More commonly it is thought that he intended the age of forty years for custom, but there is no text in which Gregory declares his choice.[44]

What, therefore, may be suggested? Did Gregory IX tolerate a custom against the law? It seems that Gregory found himself in a situation wherein he wished to tolerate certain customs of the past which had gained a foothold in the present, even against the law.

The Pontiff wishes to make provisions for such customs and yet he does not wish to relax discipline. He accomplishes both by a judicious selection of four conditions. Strictly, he legislates that there can be no custom against the natural law or even against the positive law of the Church—then, as a concession—unless the custom against the ecclesiastical law be reasonable and legitimately prescribed. Thus Pope Gregory IX safeguards the monarchy of the Church and upholds the need of papal consent for customs, a fact which was never denied absolutely. He prepares the way for the doctrine of the general consent of the ruler. In time this consent will be called legal, because it is a consent whereby a legislator gives his approval to every custom which measures up to the conditions which he states in his law. Gregory IX, therefore, gives an official admission to custom against the law.

Article 3. The *Liber Sextus* of Boniface VIII

The second official doctrine concerning custom is found in the decretals of Pope Boniface VIII. His collection, however, offers only a few points developed beyond the doctrine of Gregory IX. With Gregory, Boniface names the two qualities of custom. It must be reasonable.[45] It must be "canonically and legitimately

[44] Köstler, "Consuetudo legitime praescripta," *Zeitschrift d. Savigny-Stift.*, Kan. Abt., XXXIX (1918) 173-190.

[45] C. 1, *de censibus, exactionibus, et procurationibus*, III, 20, in VI°; c. 1, *de iureiurando*, II, 11, in VI°; c. 1, *de consuetudine*, I, 4, in VI°.

prescribed."[46] Even a custom which opposes ecclesiastical law and not the divine law may be unreasonable.[47] The juridical force of custom is shown by the many situations cited in the *Liber Sextus,* especially concerning the question of benefices.[48]

On one point only does the *Liber Sextus* of Boniface make a definite advance in the growing doctrine of customary law. It is in the question of abrogation of custom. The law reads:

> Licet Romanus Pontifex, qui iura omnia in scrinio pectoris sui censetur habere, constitutionem condendo posteriorem, priorem, quamvis de ipsa mentionem non faciat, revocare noscatur: quia tamen locorum specialium et personarum singularium consuetudines et statuta, quum sint facti et in facto consistant, potest probabiliter ignorare; ipsis, dum tamen sint rationabilia, per constitutionem a se noviter editam, nisi expresse caveatur in ipsa, non intelligitur in aliquo derogare.[49]

The common doctrine will interpret this law to mean that pontifical law abrogates all general customs contrary to it, but not a reasonable, *particular* custom, unless it be abrogated by express mention. Although the Roman Pontiff is considered to have all general laws in his legislative intent, he cannot know every patricular law or custom, and, therefore, he is not presumed to embrace them in his legislation.

Besides this law concerning the abrogation of custom, nothing further of substantial progress in the development of customary law is found in the *Liber Sextus.* One might note only a more frequent occurrence of abrogatory clauses, such as *non obstante contraria consuetudine, consuetudinibus non obstantibus, consuetudinem illam penitus improbantes.*[50]

[46] C. 9, *de officio ordinarii,* I, 16 in VI°; c. 3, *de consuetudine,* I, 4, in VI°.

[47] C. 2, *de iureiurando,* II, 11, in VI°; c. 1, *de consuetudine,* I, 4, in VI°.

[48] C. 1, *de praebendis et dignitatibus,* III, 4 in VI°; c. 13, *de electione et electi potestate,* I, 6, in VI°; c. 4, *de immunitate ecclesiarum,* III, 23, in VI°.

[49] C. 1, *de constitutionibus,* I, 2, in VI°.

[50] C. 40, *de electione et electi potestate,* I, 6, in VI°; c. un. *de clericis non residentibus in ecclesia vel praebenda,* III, 3, in VI°.

ARTICLE 4. THE *Clementinae* AND THE *Extravagantes*

Pope Clement V, the first of the Avignon Popes, adds nothing of importance to an understanding of custom in the collection of the *Corpus,* which bears his name. His compilation offers merely many examples whereby may be gathered the force and the extent of custom.[51]

Those collections of the *Corpus,* known as the *Extravagantes* may be disposed of briefly. From this source there is no substantial contribution to the doctrine of customary law.

Such is the doctrine of custom as it is found in the *Corpus Juris Canonici.* It has been shown that Gratian added little to the development of doctrine concerning custom. He did sum up well the doctrine of the past. With Gregory IX, however, there began a real growth in customary law. The promulgation of the Decretals produced commentators of the *Corpus.* These lawyers fostered greatly the study of customary law in the schools of Canon Law. And, therefore, they well merit the following chapter.

[51] C. 2, *de religiosis domibus, ut episcopo sint subiectae,* III, 11 in Clem; c. 7, *de electione et electi potestate,* I, 3, in Clem; c. 1, *de verborum significatione,* V, 11, in Clem; c. 1, *de sententia excommunicationis, suspensionis, et interdicti,* V, 10, in Clem.

CHAPTER IV

CUSTOM DURING THE AGE OF THE DECRETALISTS AND DECRETISTS

WITH the study of the Decretists and the Decretalists a developed system of customary law begins to take form. Very many questions which have been treated since, find place in the writings of those who commented on the Decretum and the Decretals.

ARTICLE 1. NOTION

A complete definition of custom is to be found only after each of its elements has developed in the course of time. Custom might be defined at this period, however, in the words of Hostiensis or of Joannes Andreae.[1]

ARTICLE 2. THE CONSENT OF THE LEGISLATOR

The Decretalists do not stress much the study of the ruler's consent, because the essential importance of the sovereign is not yet fully emphasized in the evolution of the law. It is still taught that the people, capable of making law, are the cause of custom. But the power of the people is beginning to be questioned. Sed qualiter potest populus abrogare canonem . . . cum non possit condere canonem? [2] Only a legislator can take away a law. A custom is started by private citizens. How then, it may be asked, can private citizens take away a positive law? The answer of Joannes Andreae is worthy of notice.

[1] Consuetudo est usus rationabilis competenti tempore praescriptus vel firmatus; nullo actu contrario interruptus, binario actu seu contradictorio judicio vel quod non exstet memoria, inductus, usuque communi utentium comprobatus.—Hostiensis, *Summa aurea,* lib. I, tit. IV, n. 1.

Jus quoddam illius moribus institutum qui auctoritate publica jus condere potest.—Joannes Andreae, lib. I, tit. IV, c. 1.

[2] *Glossa ad dictum ante* c. 4, D. IV *"abrogatae."*

> Fateor quod usus vel actus privatorum unius regni vel provinciae vel loci legem communem abrogare, id est ubique tollere, non possunt; sed derogare possunt in eo regno, provincia vel loco, ut sicut ibi legem municipalem facere possunt, sic et consuetudinem inducere . . . quod nec in loco id possent, *nisi quia papa vel princeps id expresse permittit* . . . Item tacite, sicut enim in alicuius praeiudicium praescribitur, et is contra quem praescribitur a iure fingitur consentire et alienare videtur, quod praescribi vel usucapi patitur . . . sic cum contra ius Ecclesiae praescribit consuetudo, iuris lator consentire videtur. Et per hoc respondetur ad id quod posset opponi, quod faciendo contra legem, per quod meretur poenam, consequi non debet quis praemium vel immunitatem.[3]

The commentators then begin to realize that custom takes its legal strength not only from the tacit consent of the community, but from the authority of the Pope's permission.[4]

There was a scholar, not a Decretalist, however, who touched everything and touched nothing which he did not embellish. It is not amiss, then, to mention briefly under various headings the thought of St. Thomas. The Angelic Doctor, as was his wont, dug deep to discover the essence of custom. His ideas will nourish an entirely different understanding of the essential element in customary law. There are two groups which can introduce law, says St. Thomas. Law may be introduced by a democracy or in a monarchy. In a democracy the ruler represents the people, the true legislator.[5] But if the society be a monarchy the ruler approves a custom.[6]

[3] Joannes Andreae, *Comment.* ad c. 11, X, I, n. 47.

[4] Panormitanus, lib. I, tit. IV, ad c. 11, n. 8.

[5] Si enim sit libera multitudo, quae possit sibi legem facere, plus est consensus totius multitudinis ad aliquid observandum, quod consuetudo manifestat, quam auctoritas principis, qui non habet potestatem condendi legem, nisi in quantum gerit personam multitudinis; unde licet singulae personae non possint condere legem, tamen totus populus condere legem potest. *Summa* I, II, Q. 97, art. 3, ad tertium.

[6] Si vero multitudo non habeat liberam potestatem condendi sibi legem, vel legem a superiori potestate positam removendi, tamen ipsa consuetudo in tali multitudine praevalens obtinet vim legis, inquantum per eos toleratur, ad quos pertinet multitudini legem imponere: ex hoc enim ipso videntur approbare, quod consuetudo introduxit. *Loc. cit.*

ARTICLE 3. THE KIND OF CONSENT IN THE SOVEREIGN

A ruler may consent to a custom in several ways. There are two kinds of consent, special and general. This general consent will later be called legal. The special consent may be given either tacitly or expressly. "When *expressed* or *tacit* consent is lacking . . . custom must be prescribed and from this time the consent of the Pope is *presumed,* or custom is approved by law." [7] This citation refers to each kind of consent. Expressed and tacit are the two kinds of special consent. The consent, which is called presumed, is general or legal approval. This legal consent is indicated by the time-element in custom.

The early Decretists and Decretalists demand that a custom obtain the special consent of the legislator. One gloss says clearly:

> Sed dic quod non potest abrogare nisi per expressum consensum Papae, licet quidam dixerint quod sufficeret sola scientia Papae.[8]

This text demands not only special consent, but expressed special consent. This is sustained by another gloss, which clearly requires special consent, if not expressed, at least tacit.

> Quod sit de scientia principis inducta, non tantum de tolerantia.[9]

Another Decretist also is satisfied with special tacit consent in the formation of custom.

> Nam nec generalis nec specialis consuetudo derogat iuri scripto, nisi ex certa scientia illius qui est auctor iuris. Item specialis consuetudo non derogat iuri scripto, nisi in eo loco in quo homines utuntur ea. . . . Cum enim papa vel imperator tacite permittat ut quaelibet ecclesia vel quilibet populus talem legem sibi condat, ipse talem legem tacito consensu videtur condere.[10]

[7] Butrius, *Repetitio,* n. 53.
[8] *Glossa ad dictum ante* c. 4, D. IV—*"abrogatae."*
[9] *Glossa ad* c. 7, D. VIII—*"consuetudinem."*
[10] Huguccio, *Summa ad* D. XI, *initio.*

Gregory IX had implied the doctrine of general or legal consent. It is not surprising then to find a Glossator writing.

> Sed credo quod consuetudo rationabilis et praescripta tollit leges etiam sine scientia principis.[11]

A consent given without the knowledge of the prince is legal consent. It is given to all customs which meet the requirements of his law, to all that are reasonable and legitimately prescribed. At least this legal consent is needed for all customs.

Some, however, are fearful of the power of custom in certain matters. They demand special consent, whenever a custom is against the public good, the sacraments, the rights of a prince, or against a law with a prohibiting clause. The legislator must know these customs, they say, and grant them special approval before they can have force. In these matters general or legal consent will not suffice. It is retorted, however, that the Decretals say nothing about such customs and Gregory IX makes no distinction whatsoever.[12]

Article 4. The Origin of Custom

For all the Decretalists a community capable of *making* law is the cause of custom. This thought prevailed until the seventeenth century. It is from the permission of a legislator that a community makes a law. "Who cannot make a law cannot induce a custom." [13] For the Decretists and the Decretalists the people are the efficient cause of custom.[14]

No definite rule is given for listing the communities capable of introducing custom. Mention is made of churches, cathedrals, cities, provinces, dioceses, chapters, monasteries. Families are properly excluded. In harmony with the note that the community capable of legislating is the only kind which can introduce custom, the commentators of this period exclude all minors, all women, all insane.[15]

[11] *Glossa ad dictum ante* c. 4, D. IV—"*abrogatae*"; ad c. 7, D. VIII—"*consuetudinem.*"

[12] Curtius, *De consuet.*, Sect. IV, n. 24, 29.

[13] Joannes Andreae, *de consuet.*, n. 13.

[14] *Glossa ad* c. 11, X, *de consuetudine,* I, 4—"*legitime praescripta.*"

[15] Panormitanus, lib. I, tit. IV, ad c. 11, n. 8; Joannes Andreae, *de consuet.*, n. 25.

The Glossators demand that a major part of the community perform the acts which introduce custom.[16] But the commentators say that it is enough if the practice of a minority be approved by the majority, with the intention of establishing law. It is said that not acts alone, but the tacit consent of the people induce custom.[17]

Article 5. The Kinds of Custom

The threefold effect of custom was thinly outlined by Gratian. The clearcut triple distinction of custom conformed to law, beside the law and against the law does not occupy the Decretalists so precisely. Indeed more than the triple effect of supplying, interpreting and abolishing law is sometimes enumerated, but the other effects named can be reduced to three.[18]

The Angelic Doctor, however, has stated well the juridical value of custom.

> Omnis lex proficiscitur a ratione et voluntate legislatoris . . . Manifestum est autem, quod verbo humano potest et mutari lex et etiam exponi, inquantum manifestat interiorem motum et conceptum rationis humanae; unde etiam et per actus maxime multiplicatos, qui consuetudinem efficiunt, *mutari potest* et *exponi,* et etiam aliquid causari, quod *legis virtutem* obtineat; . . . cum enim aliquid multoties fit, videtur ex deliberato rationis iudicio provenire: et secundum hoc consuetudo et habet *vim legis* et legem abolet, et est legum *interpretatrix.*[19]

Article 6. The Acts of the Community

The mind of the community is to be learned from the acts of the majority. But these acts must have various qualities.

[16] *Glossa ad* c. 7, D. VIII—*"consuetudinem"; Glossa ad* c. 11, X, *de consuetudine,* I, 4—*"legitime praescripta."*

[17] Panormitanus, lib. I, tit. IV, ad c. 11, n. 17.

[18] Hostiensis, *Summa aurea,* lib. I, tit. IV, n. 11; *Glossa ad* c. 7, D. XI *"pro lege," "consuetudinem";* ad c. 7, D. XII, *"contra longam";* c. 5, D. I *"cum deficit lex";* c. 7, D. VIII *"consuetudinem";* c. 4, D. XI *"vincat"; Glossa ad dictum ante* c. 4, D. IV *"abrogatae."*

[19] *Summa,* I, II, Q. 97, art. 3 concl.

(a) *The freedom of acts.* That the acts of a community must be free is a fundamental notion. Joannes Andreae notes that the force which impedes freedom is inflicted either by a private person or by a judge. If the force is produced by the former, the consent given under force is useless and the custom invalid. If the fear is caused by a judge in his capacity as a private citizen, the result is the same. But if the judge provoked fear in his juridical capacity, the consent is valid and the custom stands.[20] It is clear that lack of freedom destroys consent, which is the efficient cause of custom.

(b) *The acts should be frequent.* Concerning the number of acts the Decretalists are not in accord. It is commonly maintained that the number of acts is irrelevant. If the people, however, all at once by a kind of sudden popular impulse consent to a way of acting, no custom is formed. Only frequent successive acts produce a custom. If the legislator consents to this instantaneous will of the people, this pulse of the public indicates not customary law, but *lex.*

(c) *The acts should be uninterrupted.* Whatever the number of acts, they should be continuous. It may be that the custom has already run the course of time demanded by prescription. In this case a few interruptions, even adverse judicial sentences, make no difference; for the custom is already established as a law. On the other hand, the custom may be still running the prescribed time. In this situation a few contrary acts will not interrupt the time, but a contrary action by a majority would destroy the custom in the making.[21]

(d) *The acts should be public.* Custom may originate in actions of the people manifested juridically or extra-judicially. The acts must be public, in order that the consent and will of the people may be known. The best kind of publicity is given by court sentences. Indeed, the early commentators thought that only by a judicial sentence could custom, not immemorial, be established.

[20] Joannes Andreae, *de consuet.*, n. 28; *Glossa ad* c. 7, D. VIII—*"consuetudinem"*; *Glossa ad* c. 11, X, *de consuetudine,* I, 4—*"legitime praescripta."*

[21] Joannes Andreae, lib. I, tit. IV, c. 11, n. 30; Panormitanus, lib. I, tit. IV, ad c. 11, n. 19.

> Ad hoc ut consuetudo valeat, oportet sit obtenta contradictorio judicio id est si ex adverso negetur consuetudo. Contradictum judicium dicitur, puta cum ego dicerem hanc esse consuetudinem, adversarius dicebat non esse consuetudinem, et iudicatum fuit, quod erat consuetudo.[22]

Other glosses likewise demand this judgment *in contradictorio,* whereby a judge maintains the existence of a custom against one party who argues its non-existence. This should be an unappealed sentence.[23] Still others think that a judgment *in contradictorio* is not necessary. As long as there is a conformable decision, they say, as long as the sentence agrees with a custom, the practice attains publicity. There need be no direct affirmation of its existence. There is a difference of opinion concerning the number of sentences needed to introduce custom. Some are satisfied with two, some with ten, because, as it is said quaintly, ten sheep make a flock.[24] Panormitanus notes that some demand judicial sentences:

> Fatentur tamen doctores utriusque juris quod ex actu judiciario introducitur consuetudo: puta quia judex judicavit contra legem populo sciente et non contradicente,[25]

but he himself disagrees with the Glossators:

> Si dictum glossae esset verum, numquam posset ita introduci consuetudo, quia oportet quod habeat initium et sic numquam posset judicari pro consuetudine, quae numquam fuit obtenta in judicio.[26]

Hostiensis thinks that the judge has no intention of making his sentence bind for the future and, therefore, he doubts that custom can be established in this way.[27] It is generally admitted that court sentences proffer proof of custom, but this does not mean that they

[22] *Glossa ad* c. 25, X, *de verborum significatione,* V, 40—*"contradictorio iudicio."*

[23] *Glossa ad* c. 11, X, *de consuetudine,* I, 4—*"legitime praescripta"; Glossa ad* c. 7, D. VIII—*"consuetudinem."*

[24] Hostiensis, *Summa aurea,* lib. I, tit. IV, n. 4; *Glossa ad* c. 34, X, *de electione et electi potestate,* I, 6—*"Ex successione."*

[25] Panormitanus, lib. I, tit. IV, ad c. 11, n. 16.

[26] Panormitanus, lib. I, tit. IV, ad c. 11, n. 16.

[27] Hostiensis, *Summa aurea,* lib. I, tit. IV, n. 6.

introduce custom.[28] It is, therefore, concluded that court sentences alone cannot induce a custom. Only continued sentences, to which a majority of the people consented might introduce custom. Thus the statement of Panormitanus, cited above, concludes

> . . . populo sciente et non contradicente, unde actus iudicialis sufficit ad probandum consuetudinem, non ut actus iudiciarius sed quia per illum actum detegitur consensus populi.[29]

(e) *The intention of the community.* The earliest canonists demanded that a community have the intention of introducing a legal obligation.

> unde licet aliquid saepius factum sit, nisi eo animo factum sit ut in posterum fieret: etiam si suo jure id fieret, talis usus non dicetur usus.[30]

The same notion is found in another gloss,

> . . . eo animo ut intendas sive credas, te jus habere et ut in posterum id facias.[31]

The very reason for a time-element in custom, says Joannes Andreae, is to show the intention of the people to induce a new law.

> Sed ubi aliquid actum est, nec expressus consensus adest, nec apparet quo animo faciant, recurritur ad praesumptionem perseverantiae vel diuturnitatis . . . Sed ante diuturnum tempus non praesumitur voluisse recedere a lege scripta.[32]

The people then must use the custom with the intention of introducing a new obligation.

(f) *The question of error.* Can custom introduced by error have force? One answer states that such a custom is invalid for two reasons. It would lack the necessary consent and would be unrea-

[28] *Cf. infra* 44.

[29] Panormitanus, lib. I, tit. IV, ad c. 11, n. 16; Joannes Andreae, *de consuetudine,* n. 31-34.

[30] *Glossa ad* c. 5, D. 1—*"institutum"*; ad c. 7, D. VIII—*"consuetudinem."*

[31] *Glossa ad* c. 11, X, *de consuetudine,* I, 4—*"legitime praescripta."*

[32] Joannes Andreae, *de consuet.,* n. 37.

sonable. Custom is invalid unless reasonable . . . but if it is erroneous, it will not be reasonable, nor is it induced by consent.[33] The *Glossae* represent the same opinion. It is necessary that custom be free from error, *"non per errorem sit inducta."*[34] Another commenting on the gloss admits custom induced in error, but denies that it is to be extended to similar cases.

> Consuetudo introducta per errorem tenet quoad illum casum, sed non extenditur ad casum similem . . . Sed ubi esset tantus error, quod tolleret consensum populi, tunc procederet glossa et non esset consuetudo introducta, quia deficeret causa efficiens, scilicet ipse consensus populi.[35]

This text then would seem to admit error in custom, as long as the error is not so great that it takes away the consent of the people. This seems to contain the germ of a doctrine, which later canonists will call error *antecedens* and error *concomitans.*

(g) *Good or Bad Faith.* The glosses require that the acts which form custom be placed in good faith by the community. Later Decretalists, however, do not demand good faith. They maintain that while in prescription title and good faith are required, in custom only use and complete time are needed.[36] When it is recalled that all through this era the community was considered the *maker* of custom, it seems that there should have been no room for the question of good or bad faith in the legislator himself.

Article 7. Reasonableness

A conclusion readily reached is that no custom against the natural law could be reasonable.[37] A study of the relation between custom and the natural law is made by Panormitanus, perhaps the first of the Decretalists to develop his study free from the influence of

[33] Hostiensis, *Summa aurea,* lib. I, tit. IV, n. 7.

[34] *Glossa ad* c. 7, D. 8—*"consuetudinem"*; *Glossa ad* c. 11, X, *de consuetudine,* I, 4—*"legitime praescripta."*

[35] Panormitanus, lib. I, tit. IV, ad c. 11, n. 12.

[36] Hostiensis, *Summa aurea,* lib. I, tit. IV, n. 14; Panormitanus, lib. I, tit. IV, ad c. 8, n. 22; Joannes Andreae, lib. I, tit. IV, c. 11, n. 36.

[37] *Glossa ad* c. 11, X, *de consuetudine,* I, 4—*"rationabilis."*

Roman Law.[38] The suggestion is made that the custom must not be against morals, or the occasion of sins, or too onerous for the people.[39] One gloss suggests the same reasonableness for custom that is required for written law.[40] Hostiensis says positively that custom is reasonable, which is approved by law, which the Church keeps and commands to be observed.[41] A negative definition, however, becomes more accepted. When custom is "not reprobated by law" it is said to be reasonable.

> Illam dico rationabilem, quam non improbant iura . . . quae non obviat canonicis institutis. Irrationabilis est quae improbatur a iure . . . et onerosa consuetudo et generaliter ubi aliquid fit contra nervum ecclesiasticae disciplinae sive libertatem.[42]

If the custom is opposed to law, the presumption is against its reasonableness. A custom beside the law is more easily thought reasonable. These points a judge must decide.[43]

At an early date the question presented itself, how can a custom be reasonable, when it is against the law, which is itself reasonable? This question was clarified by the Angelic Doctor.

> Unde possibile est quandoque praeter legem agere, in casu scilicet in quo deficit lex; et tamen actus non erit malus; et cum tales casus multiplicantur propter aliquam mutationem hominum, tunc manifestatur per consuetudinem quod lex ulterius non est utilis; sicut etiam manifestaretur, si lex contraria verbo promulgaretur. Si autem adhuc maneat ratio eadem, propter quam prima lex utilis erat, non consuetudo legem, sed lex consuetudinem vincit.[44]

[38] Panormitanus, lib. I, tit. IV, ad c. 11, n. 3.

[39] *Glossa ad* c. 7, D. VIII—*"consuetudinem"*; Hostiensis, *Summa aurea,* lib. I, tit. IV, n. 3; Panormitanus, lib. I, tit. IV, ad c. 11, n. 5.

[40] *Glossa et* c. 1, *de consuetudine,* I, 4 in VI° *Casus*; *Summa,* I, II, Q. 97, art. 3; *Glossa ad* c. 7, D. I—*"jus naturale."*

[41] Hostiensis, *Summa aurea,* lib. I, tit. IV, n. 2.

[42] *Glossa ad* c. 11, X, *de consuetudine,* I, 4—*"rationabilis."*

[43] Panormitanus, lib. I, tit. IV, ad c. 11, n. 5; Hostiensis, *Summa aurea,* lib. I, tit. IV, n. 2.

[44] *Summa,* I, II, Q. 97, art. 3 ad 2.

It is well to remember that some acts are prohibited because they are evil; others are evil only because they are prohibited. When reasonableness depends upon the will of a legislator, there is nothing to prevent him from considering an action against his law as reasonable, if it measure up to the conditions placed by himself.

So, too, a Decretalist answers, if we consider one and the same end, custom contrary to law cannot be reasonable . . . but when one considers diverse ends, a custom contrary to law can also be reasonable. Two contraries can both be true, if we consider diverse ends.[45]

Another view looks at the situation not only from diverse ends but from different circumstances and time. "Nothing is so permanently good and reasonable that from circumstances and human vicissitudes it cannot be corrupted." [46]

A custom, therefore, may have the juridical value of abrogating a reasonable law and yet be reasonable itself. But if the law is strengthened by a reprobating clause, the Decretalists think that a custom cannot arise against it. To them it seems that a legal reprobation nullifies a law forever. The nullifying clause affects not only the past but also the future.[47] Whether a custom once reprobated can ever become reasonable will be considered more thoroughly by later canonists.

Article 8. The Time Required by Custom

A. Custom Against the Law

Some early canonists understood Gregory IX to mean true prescription. "That it be prescribed," they say, "it must be an object which can be prescribed." [48] Soon, however, it became clear that the time-element in custom is something distinct from real prescription. It is noted that custom concerns a majority, while prescription refers to an individual. Custom produces a right; prescription, for one party at least, extinguishes a right. Prescription demands a

[45] Panormitanus, lib. I, tit. IV, ad c. 11, c. 6.

[46] Butrius, *De consuet.*, L. 1, tit. 4, c. 11, n. 27.

[47] Panormitanus, lib. I, tit. IV, ad c. 11, n. 24.

[48] *Glossa ad* c. 11, X, *de consuetudine*, I, 4—"*legitime praescripta*"; *Glossa ad* c. 7, D. VIII.

title; no title is needed in custom.[49] When it has been fully demonstrated, under the influence of the civilists, that there can be no true prescription in custom, canonists begin to agree that a custom cannot be prescribed, because prescription concerns a law *already* formed; custom is a disposing element towards making a law, therefore, it cannot be prescribed. Yet Panormitanus retains the idea that "custom is not prescribed, but rather the law of the Pope is prescribed." [50] It is generally concluded, however, that Pope Gregory IX did not demand prescription. He merely placed a lapse of time as a juridical condition for a custom to prevail against the canons. Because individuals in the Church cannot make a statute, the canons of the Pope can be taken away by a quasi-prescription. It will be important to note henceforth that, although the words "prescription" and "legitimately prescribed" are used, the writers are not speaking of real prescription, but of this quasi-prescription, the time required in custom.

(a) An important distinction is made between a custom known to the ruler and one not known. If the ruler knows a custom and does not act against it, he is said to give *special tacit* consent to its existence. Such a custom can become law in ten years. But it must be clear that the ruler really consents, that he is not the victim of prudent silence.[51]

(b) When a custom is not known to a ruler, it is generally taught at this era that it obtains *legal* consent against the law after a duration of forty years.[52]

The *Glossae,* however, seem to demand an immemorial custom.

> Dico quod numquam de consuetudine sola (licet esset praescripta) ius aliquod sit quaesitum, nisi forte sit tanta cuius memoria non esset.[53]
> Sed longum est quod est X vel XX annorum. Non ergo

[49] Hostiensis, *Summa aurea,* lib. I, tit. IV, n. 7; *Glossa ad* c. 11, X, *de consuetudine,* I, 4—*"legitime praescripta."*

[50] Panormitanus, lib. I, tit. IV, ad c. 11, n. 7.

[51] Hostiensis, *Summa aurea,* lib. I, tit. IV, n. 5; Panormitanus, lib. I, tit. IV, ad c. 11, n. 13.

[52] Hostiensis, *Summa aurea,* lib. I, tit. IV, n. 3; Panormitanus, lib. I, tit. IV, ad c. 11, n. 11; *Glossa ad* c. 11, X, *de consuetudine,* I, 4—*"legitime praescripta."*

[53] *Glossa ad* c. 31, C. 18, q. 2— *"usque ad hoc tempus."*

> requiritur quod consuetudo excedat hominum memoriam, ut dicunt quidam, vel etiam quod sit praescripta. Sed illud verum, est, ubi consuetudo non est contra ius, vel quando est vetusta, ita ut excedat memoriam hominum . . . Item valet quia tunc habetur loco constitutionis.[54]

(c) A further old distinction is borrowed from the sources of Roman Law.[55] Some still adhered to the doctrine that a law was not confirmed until it was received by the people. The temporal duration needed for custom to abolish law was considerably shortened if that law had not yet been received in use. It is taught that a law not yet received can be abrogated through legal consent, when the contrary custom has endured but ten years, instead of the usual forty. Panormitanus says that when the custom against the unreceived law is known to the ruler, and when, therefore, he gives special consent, not even ten years are required to abolish that law.

But the distinction between a law received by the people and one not received was properly attacked. And, therefore, likewise the teaching which required only ten years or no time in such customs was opposed.[56] Yet at this time it must be admitted the opinion was common that the time needed by custom was less, when the law it opposed had not been received in use by the people.

(d) At times custom may involve the rights of some particular church, or a privilege of a prince. In such situations, where custom infringes on the rights of a third party, custom is said to be contemporaneous with prescription and forty years or time immemorial is needed. The rules of prescription must be observed.[57]

B. Custom Beside the Law

Already at this time the opinion is common that custom beside the law needs ten years duration.[58]

[54] *Glossa ad* c. 7, D. XII—"*contra longam.*"

[55] D. (1, 3) 32; *dictum post* c. 3, D. IV.

[56] Curtius, *De consuet.*, Sect. III, n. 40.

[57] Panormitanus, lib. I, tit. IV, ad c. 11, n. 11.

[58] *Glossa ad* c. 7, D. XII—"*contra longam*": "Sed longum est quod X vel XX annorum . . . Illud verum est ubi consuetudo non est contra ius"; *Glossa ad* c. 3, X, *de causa possessionis et proprietatis*, II, 12—"*de consuetudine,*" "*tertio*"; *Glossa ad* c. 31, C. XVIII, q. 2—"*usque ad hoc tempus*"; Panormitanus, lib. I, tit. IV, ad c. 11, n. 11; Joannes Andreae, *de consuet.*, n. 38.

C. Custom Conformed to Law

A custom conformed to law requires no time at all in order to be introduced.[59]

Such are the findings of the Decretalists and their age concerning the time-element in custom. The period of time demanded begins to run its course from the first act, just as soon as the acts are of such a character that they come to the notice of the greater part of the people.[60] But the exact length of time needed by custom will continue to be the subject of debate for centuries.

Article 9. Abrogation of Custom

If it be true that a new statute can abolish a former law, it is equally true that a second custom can do away with a former one. A later custom prejudices a former one if they cannot be reconciled.[61] The Decretalists, however, are not agreed concerning the duration of time needed by the second custom. One line of thought maintains that a custom must have forty years duration to abolish another custom. This opinion argues that the former custom has become law. The second is, therefore, against the law and must follow the usual rules for such a custom.[62] Another opinion, however, counters with the affirmation that the second custom is rather beside the law. And, therefore, only ten years are needed to abrogate the former contrary custom.[63] It is said that, if a custom against the law ceases to be observed by the people, the law revives without any prescribed time.[64] Such abrogation is by way of desuetude, without the introduction of a new contrary custom. Later writers will make further distinctions concerning this very question. It is clear that not only a contrary custom but also a subsequent law can take away a custom.[65]

59 Curtius, *De consuet.*, Sect. III, n. 31.

60 Joannes Andreae, *de consuet.*, n. 39.

61 Joannes Andreae, lib. I, tit. IV, ad c. 11, n. 31.

62 Curtius, *De consuet.*, Sect. IV, n. 74; III, n. 44—*Cf.* Suarez, *de leg.*, L. VII, c. 20, n. 21.

63 Panormitanus, lib. I, tit. IV, ad c. 11, n. 19.

64 Butrius, lib. I, tit. IV, c. 11, n. 20.

65 Hostiensis, *Summa aurea*, lib. I, tit. IV, n. 10.

When considering the abrogation of custom by law, the canonists of this period apply the decretal of Pope Boniface VIII.[66] They note that papal law abrogates all general contrary customs but not particular customs unless they are mentioned, because the Pope is not presumed to know them. The decretal does not speak of immemorial customs, but the commentators affirm that these customs must be mentioned in order to be included in an abrogatory law of the Pope. Such venerable customs are considered privileged and are not presumed abolished without a specific declaration.

Article 10. The Proof of Custom

The question of the proof of custom did not receive much development. Indeed before the thirteenth century it was hardly considered. There may be some indication of proof in the Decretals.[67] The more common doctrine is that custom should be proved by the one who invoked it. Hostiensis makes a rather extensive study of the methods in which this proof may be made. He enumerates four ways: (a) It could be shown that no acts contrary to the custom had been performed for a space of ten years. (b) It could be demonstrated that two judgments had been made in conformity with the custom during a long period. (c) One judgment contradicting the law in favor of custom would be another means of proof. (d) There is ample proof of custom if it be so old that in the memory of men there is nothing contrary to it.[68] It has been shown that judicial sentences are not necessary to establish a custom. Nevertheless, they do furnish a good proof that the custom has already been formed by the consent of the people.[69]

[66] *Cf. supra* 28.

[67] *Cf.* C. 25, X, *de verborum significatione,* V, 40; c. 10, X, *de officio archidiaconi,* I, 23; c. 8, X, *de consuetudine,* I, 4.

[68] Hostiensis, *Summa aurea,* lib. I, tit. IV, n. 5.

[69] The councils of this period add nothing of doctrinal importance to the developing theory of customary law. But they do take cognizance of custom as a font of law.

Cf. Mansi, *Sacrorum Conciliorum Nova et Amplissima Collectio,* XXII, 583; XXV, 301; XXVI, 384; XXXII, 1271; XXXII, 1442.

Cf. Harduinus, *Acta Conciliorum et Epistolae Decretales ac Constitutiones Summorum Pontificum,* VIII, 1009; IX, 1937.

CHAPTER V

CUSTOM DURING THE AGE OF THE DOCTORS

Article 1. Notion

The definition of Suarez is worthy of consideration. It is true that he repeats the definition of Isidore and Tertullian, "Custom is law instituted by practice, which is taken for law when law is lacking." [1] The study of the notion of custom, however, is advanced by Suarez in this way. He defends his definition by noting that custom is both a fact and a law. The definition takes care of the fact-element by the use of the word "practice." Custom of fact, however, is not law; it only leads to law. Only a custom of law has juridical value and creates an obligation which binds all. The definition, says Suarez, takes care also of this by the words, "which is taken for law." Suarez is the first to use the expression *jus consuetudinarium.*

Suarez thinks that even when a custom is written into the statute law, it still binds by force of customary law as well as by statute law. This double bond is not useless, he says, because the written law may be common, whereas the custom may be special. A privilege might derogate the former, but not the latter, except in an express way.[2]

Although the force of custom is sustained by most writers,[3] there are not lacking a few who say that the Church can have no real customary law.[4] Because custom is a kind of national conviction the thought is entirely foreign to the nature of the Church, which is international, universal. The so-called customs are not really customs. Recalling the patristic age, this line of thought affirms that

[1] Suarez, *de leg.*, L. VII, c. 1, n. 1. This definition comprises *consuetudo praeter legem* only.

[2] Suarez, *de leg.*, L. VII, c. 2, n. 4; for discussion *cf. infra* 85.

[3] Reiffenstuel, lib. I, tit. 4, n. 5; Schmalzgrueber, lib. I, tit. 4, n. 1.

[4] Puchta, *Das Gewohnheitsrecht,* II, 105.

custom is merely tradition, the deposit of faith, in action. It is the whole body of ancient practices; it is legitimate because it is time-honored.

Others, fearful for the Church and strong defenders of her monarchy, admit custom, but confine it within a very narrow field. They foresee a danger that the written law will be rendered useless by custom and that the government of the Church will be destroyed.[5] The trend of thought, however, generally follows the past and the words "*jus consuetudinarium*" come into use.[6] The notion of custom, then, is that it is "a legal right of the people introduced by usage with the consent of the legislator." [7]

Article 2. The Consent of the Sovereign

Not the least of the difficulties which canonists had to face in evaluating the binding force of custom was the part of the ruler in its formation. In this matter the study of Suarez is excellent. First of all he neatly distinguishes two efficient causes of custom. The proximate efficient cause is the people, who introduce the custom of fact. The primary efficient cause of the legal custom is the authority of the superior.[8]

Following the lead of the Angelic Doctor, Suarez then speculates on the ruler's consent in different kinds of government. If the society be a republic, the ruler is really the republic itself. The consent of the people in giving approval then embraces the consent of the ruler. If the society be an oligarchy, the consent of the people is implicitly contained in the senatorial body. In tempered monarchies the people receive from the ruler the power to make a custom. In an absolute monarchy it is certain that the ruler is the legal element which gives value to a factual custom. It alone is the essence of juridical force in customary law, for the legislative power, needed for law, is in no way possessed by the subjects

[5] Gousset, *Exposition des principes*, n. 542; Phillips, *Kirchenrecht*, L. 2, C. 2, § CLIX.

[6] Bouix, *Tract. de prin.*, p. 351, n. 6.

[7] Bauduin, *De consuet.*, n. 5.

[8] Suarez, *de leg.*, L. VII, c. 13, n. 1; Reiffenstuel, lib. I, tit. IV, n. 140, who calls the people the primary, the ruler the essential cause.

of an absolute monarchy. And, therefore, it is said that the consent of the sovereign essentially constitutes custom, so much so that without it, there would be no custom with force of law.

A departure from the traditional doctrine is later made by Phillips. Because the test of reasonableness is the spirit of the Church, the consent of the sovereign is superfluous. This, he thinks, is precisely the reason why the law *Quum Tanto* did not mention the consent of the Pope.[9]

This question of the ruler's consent is introduced by Bouix with the words, "perhaps there is no question in canonical jurisprudence which is of greater moment, or difficulty." [10] In his usual methodical way Bouix outlines his doctrine. He studies well two situations, one in which the Pope is free to speak against a custom, the other, circumstances which preclude freedom of consent. The first situation, when the Pope is free to consent, will be treated in the following number under the kind of consent. When the Pope is not free to consent, Bouix says: (1) The legislator is presumed to want his law kept, as long as it cannot be concluded that he consents to its abrogation. (2) As long as the Pope has not the facility of protesting, it cannot be concluded that he consents to a custom against the law. Bouix then distinguishes two kinds of silence. One he calls approbative, consenting silence; the other is economic, diplomatic, or prudential silence. The latter is not consent. Doctors then conclude that "however general a custom and however ancient, it cannot have the force of law without the consent of the legislator." [11] But this consent may be given in several ways.

Article 3. The Kind of Consent

(a) A ruler may consent to a custom personally or in a special way. It is, of course, supposed that the ruler knows of a custom, if he is to give this special approval. When he uses words or signs to express his approval he is said to give special *expressed* consent. When his silence alone indicates approval, because of circumstances,

[9] Phillips, *Kirchenrecht*, L. 2, C. 2, § CLXI.

[10] Bouix, *Tract. de prin.*, p. 369.

[11] Gousset, *Exposition des principes*, n. 383.

he is considered to have given special *tacit* consent. There is another kind of consent, given antecedently through the law itself. This is called legal consent.[12]

When the Pope is free to consent, Bouix considers the following possibilities: (1) If custom is *beside* the law and *certainly* reasonable, it acquires force by the simple fact that the Pope keeps silent. (2) If custom is *beside* the law and *doubtfully* reasonable, we may presume reasonableness, since the Pope, knowing it, does not protest. (3) If custom is *against* the law and *certainly* reasonable, silence gives force from the moment he is free and does not protest. (4) If custom is *against* the law and *doubtfully* reasonable, probably silence gives consent, from the hypothesis that the Pope could condemn it.[13]

Certainly personal special consent will always suffice. It is not always easy to distinguish this special consent from the prudential silence, spoken of by Bouix.[14] Special consent is needed if a custom has not existed for the prescribed time. This consent may be given either expressly or tacitly. This is true consent as long as it gives moral certitude that the sufferance of the ruler is not simple tolerance but approbation.[15]

(b) Suarez argues for the sufficiency of legal consent in this way. A custom is either prescribed or it is not prescribed. For a custom to be prescribed, Gregory IX demands only two qualities, reasonableness and a legitimate duration of time. He does not demand the personal, special consent of the legislator. Furthermore a legislator cannot possibly know every single custom, which would be necessary for personal consent. Why then can he not make a law in advance, stating under what conditions he will honor a custom? Such is legal consent.

Some, however, deny that legal consent could produce any custom.[16] They affirm that if a legislator constitutes the bar of reason, before which a custom must stand, the legislator must know the

[12] Suarez, *de leg.*, L. VII, c. 13, n. 7.

[13] Bouix, *Tract. de prin.*, p. 372.

[14] *Cf.* Suarez, *de leg.*, L. VII, c. 18, n. 16; Wernz, *Jus Decretalium*, I, n. 188.

[15] Reiffenstuel, lib. I, tit. IV, n. 95; Gousset, *Exposition des principes*, n. 384.

[16] Gousset, *Exposition des principes*, n. 385.

custom. In legal consent he cannot know the custom. Therefore special consent is always required.

Some few will not admit legal consent in a custom *beside* the law. The question of consent in this type of custom did not concern earlier writers.[17]

It seems, however, that the same power is needed to abrogate a law as to introduce one. In both kinds of custom then "the law always speaks and the will of the prince speaking through the law is not less efficacious than when it commands immediately." [18]

And therefore the most common opinion of the writers antedating the codification is that legal consent suffices. A ruler can cover in advance with the mantle of his authority a custom yet to come.[19] And just as "if some ruler decrees once and forever that he confirms all laws made by some council of prudent men, then any law of that council could have force of law, even if the prince were ignorant of it," in the same way legal consent sustains customs.[20]

The doctrine of the ruler's consent has undergone a change. No longer is it said that he permits a community to make a law, rather he gives his approbation to a custom and through him, the primary efficient cause, comes the customary law. Although the part of the sovereign is so important, although he is the efficient cause, he is not the proximate cause, for he needs the consent of the people to bring about the obligation of customary law.[21] A study of the people's part in custom follows, therefore, this consideration of the legislator's consent.

Article 4. The Community Introduces Custom

A change in the notion of the kind of community which originates custom began after the time of St. Thomas.[22] The common

[17] *Cf.* Bauduin, *De consuet.*, n. 55.

[18] Suarez, *de leg.*, L. VII, c. 13, n. 6.

[19] Bauduin, *De consuet.*, n. 54; Schmalzgrueber, lib. I, tit. 4, n. 15; Reiffenstuel, lib. I, tit. IV, n. 139; Wernz, *Jus Decretalium,* I, n. 188; Benedict XIV, *De syn. dioeces.*, lib. XIII, c. 5, n. 5.

[20] Bouix, *Tract. de prin.*, p. 384.

[21] Suarez, *de leg.*, L. VII, c. 9, n. 2.

[22] *Cf. supra* 31.

doctrine of the later writers is that the proximate cause of custom is a community *capable of receiving law*.[23] This doctrine is classic since Suarez, who made the distinction of efficient causes. The people are the proximate efficient cause, the motive cause, the quasi-occasion. "In the law of custom the people begin, in so far as it is within their power by willing, to introduce law and tacitly demand the consent of the ruler." [24] The common consent of the people then introduces custom. If the legislator consents to the acts of only a few people, the legal obligation is introduced by way of *lex*, not by way of *consuetudo*. [25]

That the people are the efficient cause of custom is affirmed by Reiffenstuel. He likewise maintains that custom draws its force only from the legal consent of the ruler. He tries to straddle these contradictory statements, but failing to make the distinction of Suarez, Reiffenstuel finally decides that the consent of the people is the only efficient cause. He seems to introduce the consent of the ruler only under pressure.[26] The common opinion, however, remains that the people merely present the material of custom; the consent of the ruler gives the force of law.[27]

There is much speculation concerning the particular kinds of communities which can introduce custom. Suarez is content to say that custom must be introduced by a perfect community, capable of receiving law.[28] Among the list are numbered cities, parishes, cathedral chapters, towns, dioceses. Families are excluded.[29] Since it has been established that a community is not a legislator, the right of women to introduce custom is defended.[30] Heretics could establish a custom, but it would not be reasonable and, therefore, would have no force of law.[31]

[23] Suarez, *de leg.*, L. VII, c. 9, n. 9; Reiffenstuel, lib. I, tit. IV, n. 110.
[24] Suarez, *de leg.*, L. VII, c. 12, n. 1.
[25] Suarez, *de leg.*, L. VII, c. 9, n. 12; Bauduin, *De consuet.*, n. 84.
[26] *Cf.* Reiffenstuel, lib. I, tit. IV, n. 125, as compared with n. 140.
[27] Schmalzgrueber, lib. I, tit. IV, n. 3.
[28] Suarez, *de leg.*, L. VII, c. 3, n. 10.
[29] Reiffenstuel, lib. I, tit. IV, n. 110.
[30] Suarez, *de leg.*, L. VII, c. 9, n. 11.
[31] Reiffenstuel, lib. I, tit. IV, n. 145.

Article 5. The Juridical Value of Custom

(a) Custom conformed to law. Suarez affirms that custom can interpret law in a double way. It may give a *doctrinal* interpretation in so far as a popular observance is a witness to the mind of the legislator. Such interpretation is not infallible, but it does give a very strong probability concerning the law's meaning. When on the other hand a practice enjoys all the conditions needed for establishing a customary law, it can produce an *authentic* interpretation, which gives all the certitude of law. This distinction of Suarez will be helpful in interpreting later the rule of law which is found in the Code, *consuetudo est optima interpres.*[32]

The school of law which fears custom is willing, nevertheless, to recognize a custom conformed to law. In such a custom nothing more is seen than an interpretation of the deposit of Christianity.[33]

(b) Custom beside the law. Where there is no written law, a custom often originates. Suarez points out that custom always originates with the people and that it is not to be confused with practices which are the result of ancient statute laws. A tradition which is the product of individual authority and not of the people still represents the voice of the sovereign.[34]

Even those who frown on custom are willing to tolerate custom beside the law. For them it is a mere development of the divine deposit.[35] It may be said, however, that a custom beside the law is admitted by all the doctors and has "force of law binding not only for the external, but also for the internal forum." It may even introduce penalties.[36]

(c) Custom against the law. This is always the most important study concerning custom. At this time it is well established that there can be a custom against the law, if it be clothed with the conditions enumerated throughout these pages. Suarez sums up the ques-

[32] Suarez, *de leg.*, L. VII, c. 17, n. 2; c. 4, n. 14; Reiffenstuel, lib. I, tit. IV, n. 151; *cf. supra* 64 and 130.

[33] Phillips, *Kirchenrecht*, L. 2, C. 2, § CLX.

[34] Suarez, *de leg.*, L. VII, c. 4, n. 10.

[35] Phillips, *Kirchenrecht*, L. 2, C. 2, § CLX.

[36] Reiffenstuel, lib. I, tit. IV, n. 158; Suarez, *de leg.*, L. VII, c. 16, n. 3; Bauduin, *De consuet.*, n. 161, 162.

tion well. He says that the establishment of such a custom is within both the power and the will of the people and the ruler. It is certainly within the power of the people to start a custom of fact by the simple course of not obeying the law. The ruler clearly has the power to consent to this action or lack of action on the part of the people. The sovereign need not make himself subservient to the people, so that his legislation depends on the pleasure of the people. Such a situation would be the downfall of all rule and order. But there is nothing to prevent him from giving juridical value of his own free will to a popular usage. It is also possible that both ruler and people have the will to create a custom against the law. The people express their intention and will by the fact that a majority departs from the law. The ruler need but add his consent, which he may do in ways indicated elsewhere.[37]

The school of thought which allows a custom conformed to law and tolerates a custom beside the law, while frowning on its wide acceptance, absolutely disdains a custom against the law. "Every custom contrary to the law of the Church is contrary to reason. This opposition implies an indirect opposition with the divine law." [38]

It has been objected that either the law must be evil or the custom against it must be unreasonable. But it is answered that as long as the consent of the ruler is present, a custom against the law need not be irrational.[39] For "though some church law is good and useful for the generality of the church, a contrary custom flourishing somewhere can be more useful for that region on account of special circumstances. And if it were not more useful it would not be evil by nature, just as a new law abrogating an old one does not suppose that the former law was evil, but only that it is no longer as equally useful as the contrary law." [40] So, too, Suarez reasons that custom against the law is not of necessity intrinsically evil, but more often extrinsically evil, and this depends on the will of a legislator, who can take away that malice.[41] A law ceases to oblige, when the circum-

[37] Suarez, *de leg.*, L. VII, c. 18, n. 4, 5.
[38] Phillips, *Kirchenrecht*, L. 2, C. 2, § CLXIII.
[39] Bauduin, *De consuet.*, n. 99.
[40] Bouix, *Tract. de prin.*, p. 363.
[41] Suarez, *de leg.*, L. VII, c. 6, n. 4.

stances for which it was framed no longer exist, that is, when it becomes unreasonable.[42]

2. *Custom Against Certain Special Laws*

(a) Although it has been established that custom can abolish law, there is some hesitancy at this period of development concerning certain laws. Canonists are slow to say that custom can abrogate the diriment impediments of matrimony. They recall the decretals [43] which declare such customs to be corruptions of law. It soon becomes clear that even these customs can be reasonable. The difference of opinion, however, survived down to the Code.[44]

(b) Must it be said moreover that any *lex irritans vel inhabilitans* can never be opposed by custom? Even these can be abrogated by custom. It is clear that acts placed contrary to these laws are null and void in their legal sphere, but by their very nature they remain acts capable of introducing custom. Even they may be reasonable.[45]

(c) Nay more! A custom can abolish even a law to which there is attached a canonical sanction. An *ipso facto* penalty would probably dissuade popular action against the law, but it is not impossible that a community ignore the penalty, while a legislator condones its acts.[46]

All these laws, which seem so rigorous, are no exception to the principles of customary law. It is always possible that custom contrary to them may be reasonable. There may be in given circumstances a good cause for relaxing the tenacity of the law.[47] Only when acts are not reasonable from any point of view whatsoever

[42] Suarez, *de leg.*, L. VII, c. 18, n. 23; *cf. supra* 39, *Summa* I, II, Q. 97, art. 3, ad 2.

[43] C. 3, X, *de cognatione spirituali*, IV, 11; c. 5, X, *de consanguinitate et affinitate*, IV, 14.

[44] Bauduin, *De consuet.*, n. 362-397; *cf.* Canon 1041, which reprobates such customs.

[45] Suarez, *de leg.*, L. VII, c. 19, n. 13; Bauduin, *De consuet.*, n. 172.

[46] Bauduin, *De consuet.*, n. 168.

[47] Suarez, *de leg.*, L. VII, c. 19, n. 2; Bauduin, *De consuet.*, n. 169.

can it be said that they will never create a custom. Presuming, therefore, the consent of the legislator and the other necessary qualities of custom, studied in these pages, it seems that any acts, not intrinsically evil, have the possibility of introducing a custom.

(d) Custom and the Council of Trent. It was at one time denied that custom could abolish any decrees of the Council of Trent. Those who feared any custom especially upheld this doctrine.[48] On the other side it has been claimed that custom can rise against the Tridentine laws similarly as against any others.[49] No arguments seem capable of proving that a custom cannot abolish the laws of this council, which, after all, was partly disciplinary in its acts. It cannot be demonstrated that customs against the Council of Trent are of necessity unreasonable. The decree of Pope Pius IV, *Benedictus Deus,* which confirms the council does not contain any clause which reprobates all future customs contrary to Trent. Nor does the constitution *In principis apostolorum* which revokes privileges contrary to the council, reprobate all customs.[50]

Within the decrees of the council itself there cannot be found any clause which prohibits or reprobates all contrary customs. There are, however, certain individual laws which may reprobate customs contrary to their specific enactments.[51]

It may be admitted that it will be more difficult for custom to abolish the laws of the Council of Trent. But that every custom against the council is not unreasonable can be gathered from the decisions of the Rota and the Sacred Congregation of the Council which have admitted some customs.[52]

[48] Gousset, *Exposition des principes,* nn. 408-430.

[49] Bouix, *Tract. de princ.,* p. 399; Wernz, *Jus Decretalium,* I, n. 194; Bauduin, *De consuet.,* n. 251, who gives an entire *Pars Specialis* to the question.

[50] *Benedictus Deus,* 25 Jan., 1564; *In principis Apostolorum,* 17 Feb., 1565. *Cf. Canones et Decreta Concil. Trid.,* p. 283, 1904 edition.

[51] Bauduin, *De consuet.,* n. 318.

[52] *ASS,* VII, 379; XII, 492; XIII, 264. For a complete study of this question—*cf.* Biederlack, "Die Gewohnheiten gegen die Disziplinardekrete des Trienter Konsils," *Zeitschrift fur katholische Theologie,* VI (1882), 438-471; Bauduin, *Pars Specialis,* n. 251-361.

Cf. supra 120 for a phase of this question after the Code.

Article 6. The Acts of the Community

Many are the qualities needed in the acts of the community which introduces custom.

(a) The acts must first of all be free. Unless the community places acts freely, it would hardly have the intention of introducing custom.[53] It can be said also that the ruler would not give his consent to acts performed by his people under force.[54]

(b) The acts should be also uniform and frequent. Uniformity of action is necessary to produce a norm. There is, however, some dispute concerning the frequency and number of acts needed. Some maintain that no definite number of acts is required, as long as there is frequency; [55] another is satisfied with one notorious act; [56] another lets the judge decide the number of acts.[57] The uniformity of the numerous acts is, of course, to be computed morally. A few contrary acts by a minority do not destroy the growing custom.

(c) These frequent acts should be also continuous. The succession is broken when a superior punishes a transgressor, when a judge decides in favor of the law against the custom, when the majority of people themselves begin to act contrary to the evolving custom. If, however, the time of prescription has already run its course, the custom is already established as law. Only a new contrary custom could abolish it.[58]

(d) The acts must be public. They may be public either in fact or in law. The opinion of the older canonists demanded publicity of law or judicial sentences,[59] but Suarez refutes that teaching in this way. Tersely he reasons, if a custom needs a sentence to confirm it, it is not yet a perfect custom. A court judgment will not supply what it lacks. But if the custom is already perfected,

[53] Reiffenstuel, lib. I, tit. IV, n. 127; Schmalzgrueber, lib. I, tit. IV, n. 14; Suarez, *de leg.*, L. VII, c. 12, n. 1, c. 5, n. 14.

[54] Suarez, *de leg.*, L. VII, c. 12, n. 11; Gousset, *Exposition des principes*, n. 367; Bouix, *Tract. de prin.*, p. 360.

[55] Suarez, *de leg.*, L. VII, c. 10, n. 3.

[56] Reiffenstuel, lib. I, tit. IV, n. 119.

[57] Schmalzgrueber, lib. I, tit. IV, n. 33.

[58] Bauduin, *De consuet.*, n. 157.

[59] *Cf. supra* 35.

with all its necessary conditions, the judgment will not be necessary. Suarez thinks the acts should have publicity of fact in order to obtain the consent of the ruler, but he rightly denies the need of judicial publicity.[60] Yet some later writers think that two court sentences, which have not been appealed, show the tacit consent of the people to a custom.[61] This relationship of judicial sentences to custom is aptly stated by Bauduin.

1. If the judge is not a legislator, even a long series of sentences by him will not make law. It may, however, enjoy the authority of jurisprudence.

2. If the judge is also the legislator, one sentence makes law, not customary, but statute law. Nevertheless if a custom is almost perfected, and by a sentence a legislator gives his tacit consent, it might be considered as customary law.

3. If the people, nevertheless, adapt themselves to the judgments, then the sentences can induce law not of their own power, but by force of the people's custom.[62]

(e) The Intention Needed by the Community.

1. *Intention in Acts Against the Law.* Acts alone do not suffice to make custom. It is necessary that they be done with the intention of inducing custom. This intent is ordinarily implicit rather than expressed.[63] This intention need not tend directly to establish a new legal custom, but it may be the mere wish not to have a certain law, to return to a former discipline, to be free from obligation in a certain matter.[64] The very custom of fact indicates the will of the people to abolish the law.[65] This is a kind of petition for the legislator's approval. The ruler approves and confirms what the people intend.[66]

It has been claimed, however, that no intention is needed in

[60] Suarez, *de leg.*, L. VII, c. 11, n. 4; c. 10, n. 5; *cf.* Michiels, *Normae Generales*, II, p. 50, note 4.

[61] Reiffenstuel, lib. I, tit. IV, n. 176; Bouix, *Tract. de prin.*, p. 352.

[62] Bauduin, *De consuet.*, n. 91; Suarez, *de leg.*, L. VII, c. 11, nn. 10-14; Wernz, *Jus Decretalium*, I, n. 187, II.

[63] Suarez, *de leg.*, L. VII, c. 12, n. 11.

[64] Suarez, *de leg.*, L. VII, c. 14, n. 6; Wernz, *Jus Decretalium*, I, n. 190, II.

[65] Suarez, *de leg.*, L. VII, c. 14, n. 8; c. 15, n. 10.

[66] Suarez, *de leg.*, L. VII, c. 12, n. 1.

custom contrary to law because such acts are not committed with the will to abrogate law, since the force and the authority of custom as law issues not from the will of the subjects, but from the ruler.[67] It may be admitted that the consent of the legislator is the formal cause of the law's abrogation. Nevertheless in custom the people anticipate the ruler and ask his consent to the abrogation. Only when they intend to abolish law is there a custom.[68]

2. *Intention in Acts Beside the Law.* It is noted that in custom beside the law, there is more need to manifest the intention of producing an obligation, because the legislator is not presumed to impose a new obligation on the people, unless they themselves wish to oblige themselves to a new custom.[69] If intention were not needed in acts beside the law, people would be burdened with countless obligations. Many acts are performed without any intention to produce a law. The recitation of the Angelus, thrice a day, the use of holy water at the church door, the use of the palms and the ashes of Lent, are not binding under law.[70]

Suarez admits that it is not easy to prove the existence of this intention in customs beside the law. People are not prone to shoulder additional burdens. It would seem then that many acts are done only out of devotion. There are, nevertheless, certain indications that the intention has produced a custom of law. When the majority have kept a difficult custom for a long time, when the prudent are scandalized at its non-observance, when transgressors of the custom are punished, when the custom clearly benefits the common good to a very great extent—these are indications that a custom exists.[71] More commonly the doctors conclude in demanding intention both for custom against the law and beside the law.[72]

(f) The Question of Error.

1. *Error in Acts Against the Law.* (a) The classical treatise

[67] Zallinger, *Institutiones,* lib. I, tit. IV, §§ 234-237.

[68] Bauduin, *De consuet.*, n. 126; Suarez, *de leg.*, L. VII, c. 14, n. 5.

[69] Bouix, *Tract. de prin.*, p. 361.

[70] Bauduin, *De consuet.*, n. 131; Suarez, *de leg.*, L. VII, c. 14, n. 5; Reiffenstuel, lib. I, tit. IV, n. 129.

[71] Suarez, *de leg.*, L. VII, c. 15, n. 13.

[72] Schmalzgrueber, lib. I, tit. 4, n. 14.

of Suarez does not fail to treat the question of error. For him any kind of error prevents the introduction of custom, because it prevents intention.[73] Suarez maintains the need of intention for customs both against the law and beside the law, and, therefore, considers freedom from error a necessary accompaniment in the formation of both kinds of customary law. Error clearly destroys intention in a custom against the law. People acting against a law, which does not command what they think, cannot intend to derogate that law.[74]

(b) Others admit that there can be an error of law underlying a custom with force of law. When the people know of an existing law, but judge erroneously concerning the scope of its application, then their error is designated as error of law. When, however, the people think that there is a law, where there is not, the error is called an error of fact. Only *error juris* and not *error facti* is admitted by this opinion in the formation of custom.[75]

(c) The doctrine concerning error which was due to gain the most popularity up to the codification may be expressed in this way. Although man may be prone to evil from his youth, there are some laws which are so manifestly good, that once known, they would be accepted by all. If through ignorance or error man should not know these laws, yet he has within himself an interpretative intention, whereby he would wish to obey them, if he did know. Likewise some laws are patently useless, if not evil, in given circumstances. A man may not know that the law exists, yet even in his error he may be said to have an intention of abolishing a useless law, if he knew of its existence. His action against the law indicates this. Such is the doctrine of concomitant error and intepretative intent.[76]

2. *Error in Acts Beside the Law.* The more general opinion of canonists at this time excludes error in custom which supplies law. But a contrary opinion admits the presence of some error. "If the error, by which the people think a law exists, is the sole cause of a

[73] Suarez, *de leg.*, L. VII, c. 12, nn. 4, 5.

[74] Reiffenstuel, lib. I, tit. IV, n. 126; Schmalzgrueber, lib. I, tit. IV, n. 14; Gousset, *Exposition des principes*, n. 367.

[75] Laymann, *Ius can.*, L. I, tit. IV, c. 11, n. 10; Pirhing, *Ius can.*, L. I, tit. IV, nn. 25, 26.

[76] Bauduin, *De consuet.*, n. 125.

practice, then the intention of the people to induce an obligation is lacking. But if the error were only concomitant, so that, if the people were to know of the law's non-existence, they would wish that it did exist, then the intention is not lacking and the law is induced by custom." [77] This is the same doctrine of the interpretative intention given for custom against the law. Error, called antecedent, being the sole cause of a custom prevents the needed intent, but error, called concomitans, does not destroy intention. In other words, if the sole cause of action is erroneus, there can be no intention, but if the error accompanies other causes for action, there may be intent.[78]

(g) Good and Bad Faith in Custom. It is clear that the question of good or bad faith concerns only a custom against the law. A custom conformed to law or beside the law will always involve good faith.

(a) Some have held tenaciously to the need of good faith. They have been influenced, it seems, by the doctrine of real prescription, which requires good faith. Further, they think acts in bad faith are sins and, therefore, unreasonable, and incapable of producing law.[79]

(b) Suarez and others affirm that the first acts of a growing custom against the law must be placed in bad faith, but he would not maintain that all consequent acts must be evil. "Successors can presume that the law was not kept for some reasonable cause, which indeed, is very likely, especially when abrogation is made through long prescription." [80]

(c) Still others say that "it is morally impossible for subjects in the beginning not to know that they act against the law." [81] Therefore, they say, good faith is not required. On the other hand, bad faith is not absolutely necessary because, "when a legislator has

[77] Bauduin, *De consuet.*, n. 134.

[78] Bauduin, *De consuet.*, n. 130; Wernz, *Jus Decretalium*, I, n. 190, II.

[79] Laymann, *Theol. mor.*, L. I, tract. IV, c. 24, n. 11; Pirhing, *Jus can.*, L. I, tit. 4, n. 44.

[80] Suarez, *de leg.*, L. VII, c. 18, n. 24; Schmalzgrueber, L. I, tit. 4, n. 25; Bouix, *Tract. de prin.*, pp. 380-382.

[81] Reiffenstuel, lib. I, tit. IV, n. 143.

failed to obtain his end, wisely and properly yielding to the weakness of his subjects, his purpose is considered revoked, at least by legal and juridical consent, notwithstanding the evil end of his subjects, who before this time sinned through a transgression of law." [82] Furthermore, it is prudent for a legislator to yield to customs even if there should be bad faith. There is less evil in yielding than in sustaining an intolerable law, which causes many to sin against it. He does not thus encourage sin or laxity. He can always check transgressions by punishments. By vigilance the legislator can always interrupt a custom, which might upset authority; he can deny it juridical consent.[83] Out of these various opinions the doctrine prevailed that neither good nor bad faith is needed.[84] These qualities were once demanded by the decretalists to evidence the consent of the people, which was thought to be the efficient cause of custom. With the development of doctrine, however, the same qualities come to be required merely as evidence that the people are using the custom.

Article 7. The Quality of Reasonableness

Suarez gives his own rule for judging the reasonableness of custom. Suppose, says he, that custom were reduced to written law. Ask yourself what are the conditions that this law be just? Apply the very same qualifications to custom. But there Suarez leaves the matter, like a rhetorical question, and says nothing about what these qualities should be.[85] Perhaps Phillips has best stated the concept of legal reasonableness. To be reasonable custom must conform to the spirit of Christianity. The Church is always on her guard lest custom violate the fundamentals of Christ's doctrine. And, therefore, whatever is contrary to the end and the purpose of the Church is contrary to reason.[86]

A custom against the law need not be so evidently reasonable as a custom beside the law.[87] The reason for this statement is that in

[82] Reiffenstuel, lib. I, tit. IV, n. 144.

[83] Bauduin, *De consuet.*, n. 128.

[84] Wernz, *Jus Decretalium*, n. 190, II.

[85] Suarez, *de leg.*, L. VII, c. 6, nn. 5-9; Wernz, *Jus Decretalium*, I, n. 190, III.

[86] Phillips, *Kirchenrecht*, L. 2, C. 2, § CLXIII.

[87] Suarez, *de leg.*, L. VII, c. 18, n. 9.

a custom against the law, there is a greater presumption that the law itself is unreasonable.[88] There should be some reasonable cause for changing the law.[89] Others think that a custom beside the law or conformed to law is clearly reasonable. But a custom against the law is to be suspected.[90]

It is within the power of a legislator to say that any custom contrary to his law is unreasonable. According to Suarez this condemnation can be one of two kinds. The lawmaker may declare that a practice is from its very nature patently unreasonable *forever.* Such a custom is intrinsically evil. On the other hand he may condemn a custom, which is not in its nature irrational, and he may decree that such a practice, as far as the law is concerned, must be considered unreasonable, for *the present* circumstances.[91] This condemnation of a custom as unreasonable by a reprobatory clause, must be distinguished from a mere prohibition or abrogation.[92]

Article 8. Time Required for Custom

A break from the historical line of thought concerning prescription is made by Suarez. Departing from the past he separates the time-element from custom. For him "legitimately prescribed" means only that a custom has the conditions demanded by law.[93] Time, for Suarez, is not an essential element of custom. Theoretically he cannot be proved wrong, but historically and practically he has disregarded the time-honored interpretation of Gregory IX, which demanded of custom two qualities, reason and prescription.[94]

Phillips retreated from the doctrine of Suarez to the traditional understanding of the Decretals. The time-element is an essential note of custom. It is not, however, a real prescription, but a lapse of time

[88] Suarez, *de leg.*, L. VII, c. 6, n. 15; Reiffenstuel, lib. I, tit. IV, n. 35.

[89] Suarez, *de leg.*, L. VII, c. 18, n. 10.

[90] Schmalzgrueber, lib. I, tit. IV, n. 7.

[91] Suarez, *de leg.*, L. VII, c. 19, n. 24; Schmalzgrueber, lib. I, tit. IV, n. 23; Reiffenstuel, lib. I, tit. IV, nn. 45, 46.

[92] Bauduin, *De consuet.*, n. 19.

[93] Suarez, *de leg.*, L. VII, c. 8, n. 1—*Cf.* Köstler, *ZSS*, XXXIX (1918), 154-194.

[94] Suarez, *de leg.*, L. VII, c. 8, n. 12.

which bars action. "Prescription is not taken in its usual acceptation . . . the whole analogy between prescription in custom and that needed for the acquisition or loss of private goods is reduced to a certain interval of time." [95] Time must be considered in reference to the various kinds of custom.

A. *Custom Against the Law*

1. Suarez speaks of time, but not as a true prescription. He demands time of a custom before it can derogate the rights of the Church. When a custom is known to a legislator no definite time is required, because the ruler gives *special* consent.[96] Reiffenstuel sustains the opinion of Suarez and notes that when the personal consent of the legislator is *expressed,* no definite time is required, for this consent has already revoked the law contrary to custom. If the personal special consent is *tacit,* a determined time is likewise useless for the law is already suppressed by the tacit revocation of the legislator, not indeed by way of prescription, but by way of connivance.[97]

2. But when a custom is not known to a ruler and when, therefore, it requires *legal* consent, forty years are necessary for it to prevail against the law. Of itself this time, says Suarez, is not of the essence of custom, but it assures the ruler's consent.[98]

Against Suarez, the opinion is offered that ten years are enough to establish any custom with legal consent.[99] Reiffenstuel rejects the notion of real prescription in the decretal *Quum Tanto* of Gregory. Therefore he sees no reason for requiring forty years' duration and he thinks that ten years suffice for custom to abolish any law whatsoever. Ten years' duration represented the more common opinion up to the codification.

Still another notion is found in Gousset. He would fix no definite

[95] Phillips, *Kirchenrecht,* L. 2, C. 2, § CLXII.

[96] Suarez, *de leg.,* L. VII, c. 15, n. 8; c. 18, n. 17.

[97] Reiffenstuel, lib. I, tit. IV, n. 93.

[98] Suarez, *de leg.,* L. VII, c. 18, n. 12.

[99] Bauduin, *De consuet.,* n. 150; Reiffenstuel, lib. I, tit. IV, n. 101; Schmalzgrueber, lib. I, tit. IV, n. 9; Benedict XIV, *De Syn. dioeces.,* 1. XIII, c. 5, n. 4; Bouix, *Tract de prin.,* p. 389.

time for custom but would leave its determination in each instance to prudent judgment.[100]

3. It should be remembered that sometimes a case presents a mixture of custom and prescription. Whenever the right of a third individual is involved, the rule of real prescription should be followed, and more than ten years would be required. So Reiffenstuel notes that the examples used in defense of a forty years' norm concern benefices, church immovables, or the rights of a prince. Even Rota decisions, cited to uphold the forty year doctrine, are always such as concern the *jus quaesitum* of a third party.[101]

4. Suarez makes a further distinction when considering custom against the law. In some strange way he still retained, it seems, the ancient notion of a law received and a law not received. When a custom runs counter to a law not yet received in use, not even ten years are needed, but only enough time that the will of the ruler be made known, his will to free the people from the obligation of the law.[102] At this period of development, however, it was becoming clear that no distinction should be made between a law received by the people and one not received. Suarez himself, therefore, mindful of the importance of the legislator's consent, which he calls the essence of custom, hesitates to distinguish a law received from one not received by the people. Rightly, therefore, is his distinction attacked.[103]

B. Custom Beside the Law

1. For a custom beside the law Suarez demands ten years, simply because custom must have the appearance of long time, which could hardly be below ten years. Whether the legislator be present or absent matters not; if he does not know a custom, he is absent in intention.[104] It may be remarked that those who demand ten years for a custom contrary to law follow Suarez here and say that

[100] Gousset, *Exposition des principes*, n. 382.

[101] Reiffenstuel, lib. I, tit. IV, n. 109; Schmalzgrueber, lib. I, tit. IV, n. 10.

[102] Suarez, *de leg.*, L. IV, c. 16, n. 12; L. VII, c. 18, n. 12.

[103] Reiffenstuel, lib. I, tit. IV, n. 102; Bauduin, *De consuet.*, n. 147 and n. 230.

[104] Suarez, *de leg.*, L. VII, c. 15, n. 5.

ten years suffice also for a custom beside the law, when it has legal consent.[105]

Naturally those who require no definite time for a custom contrary to law do not demand temporal duration in a custom beside the law. They argue that if there is no true prescription, one cannot set a definite time for a custom to be established by legal consent.[106]

2. When a custom beside the law receives the *special* consent of the legislator, it is affirmed that less than ten years are required to introduce the custom.[107] It seems that there must be some passage of time otherwise the law would be from the will of the legislator and not from the customary acts of the people, but it is taught that *no determined* duration can be set down when a custom beside the law is known to the ruler and receives his special consent.[108]

C. *Custom Conformed to Law*

Suarez denies that custom strictly conformed to a clear law is a real legal custom. It can be nothing more than a custom of fact, which brings with it no new obligation and therefore requires no prescribed time.[109] But if the law is doubtful and the application of it by the community has assumed all the qualities needed for customary law, then the popular interpretation is authentic in the sense that it will be recognized by the legislator. If the interpretation of the community either substantially extends or restricts the law, the custom must be likened to a custom beside the law or against the law. In either situation the duration of time needed for that kind of custom must be fulfilled.

D. *Prohibitory Clauses*

Some laws contain clauses forbidding contrary customs. The question was asked, therefore, if a custom could be prescribed against

[105] Bauduin, *De consuet.*, n. 144; Reiffenstuel, lib. I, tit. IV, n. 91; Wernz, *Jus Decretalium*, I, n. 190, IV; Bouix, *Tract. de prin.*, p. 387.

[106] Kreutzwald, *De canon.*, p. 87; Sägmüller, *Lehrbuch*, p. 79.

[107] Suarez, *de leg.*, L. VII, c. 15, n. 8.

[108] Bauduin, *De consuet.*, n. 136; Wernz, *Jus Decretalium*, I, n. 190, IV.

[109] Suarez, *de leg.*, L. VII, c. 17, n. 2.

such a law, and if so, was there a different length of time required. There is no question here of a revocatory clause which concerns past customs and is considered under the caption of "abrogation." [110] Nor is this a question of a reprobatory phrase, which condemns a custom as unreasonable and which has been noted under the heading of "reasonableness." [111] With this in mind Suarez notes that a prohibiting clause does not condemn a custom as unreasonable. It refers only to future customs, which might arise against the law. It might indeed embrace the customs existing when the law was made, but this would have to be indicated clearly. One opinion maintains that custom can abrogate a law with a prohibitory clause by the same length of time as that which is demanded to abolish any law.[112] But the more common opinion declares that a law with a prohibitory clause can be abolished only by a custom which is centenary or immemorial, or by the special consent of the legislator.[113]

Article 9. Abrogation of Custom

A custom may be abrogated either by another custom or by a statute law. Each means will be considered in turn.

(a) By another custom. If law can be abolished by custom, it is equally true that one custom can be abrogated by another custom. This implies that a reconciliation between the two customs cannot be effected; they must be really contrary one to the other. There is a divergence of opinion concerning the length of time required by the second custom, in order that it abolish the first.

1. Suarez answers the question with a distinction. The first custom, he reasons, has either totally abolished the old law or it has not. If the written law has been completely abrogated in a given locality, customary law prevails there. Therefore, a second custom, arising contrary to the existing practice is *praeter legem scriptam* but it is *contra jus consuetudinarium,* which has supplanted the written law. Forty years are needed then to abrogate the first custom.

110 *Cf. infra* 68.

111 *Cf. supra* 61.

112 Suarez, *de leg.*, L. VII, c. 19, n. 18.

113 Bauduin, *De consuet.*, n. 173; Reiffenstuel, lib. I, tit. IV, n. 47; Wernz, *Jus Decretalium,* I, n. 191, III.

But if the written law has not been totally abrogated within a given territory, continues Suarez, a second custom, which is contrary to the former usage, really effects a return to the old written law. This second custom can abolish a former contrary custom without any prescribed time.[114]

Bauduin, however, takes a different view. If the first custom is considered *praeter legem* a second contrary to it is also *praeter legem,* because it abrogates a situation which is beside the law. And if the first custom is *contra legem,* the second is again *praeter legem* because the old law has been abrogated by custom. For the abrogation of custom in this circumstance ten years' time suffices.[115] Schmalzgrueber expresses the opinion that the second custom requires the same length of time to abolish a custom as that first custom itself took to become law.[116]

2. A somewhat different situation is contemplated by Suarez. Let it be supposed that a law has never been carried out by the people, that they have never received it in use and there is a custom of disobedience against it. The law itself has gone into desuetude. Later the community begins to reëstablish the old law. Must the people act for forty or ten years in order to revive the law, which they have disobeyed so long? This opinion states that the second custom can abolish the desuetude without any determined time. The law has been suspended, as it were, during the first custom of disobedience and the law returns to use without a fixed time.[117]

3. There is a final hypothesis. Suppose that a law has been received and obeyed by the people. In due time they introduce a custom which abrogates the law they once followed. The community later begins to disregard the custom. Does the old law revive? Bouix is of the opinion that no time is required to abolish the former custom. The legislator, says Bouix, always desires a return to his law. As soon as the people cease to act against it, their custom ceases, and the law is resurrected.[118] There seems to be no proof

[114] Suarez, *de leg.*, L. VII, c. 20, n. 21.

[115] Bauduin, *De consuet.*, n. 223.

[116] Schmalzgrueber, lib. I, tit. IV, n. 38.

[117] Suarez, *de leg.*, L. IV, c. 16, n. 13.

[118] Bouix, *Tract. de prin.*, p. 410.

of this assumption but it would be true, if the special consent of the ruler is given. These distinctions concerning the time needed by one custom to abolish another will lose their importance with the advent of the Code of Canon Law.

(b) Abrogation by law. A custom may be abrogated also by law. If the legislator directly revokes his consent, the custom is abrogated immediately. But, suppose the lawmaker produces a law that is contrary to a custom only indirectly does he wish thereby to revoke the custom? The main study of this question has been to interpret the official doctrine of Pope Boniface VIII. He states that a law abrogates a general custom without mentioning it, but not a particular custom unless it be mentioned.

Suarez says that there must be a real opposition between the law and the custom, otherwise they are to be reconciled. "A correction of law should be avoided, of custom all the more so, because custom, as it were, has become ingrafted in nature, and so it is difficult to change, also because laws should be accommodated to the usages of the users." [119] Doctors conclude from the law of Pope Boniface: (a) that a universal law revokes a *general* contrary custom without mentioning it. (b) That a universal law must mention a *particular* contrary custom to abrogate it. (c) That a special law for a particular place derogates a contrary custom without mention. It may be noted that the logic of the law of Pope Boniface depends upon a presumption of knowledge. The Pope is presumed to know all general contrary customs; he is not presumed to have in mind particular customs, unless he mentions them. This same reasoning also makes clear that the law regards papal legislation only. It does not apply to an inferior, a bishop. A lesser legislator with a more limited jurisdiction is presumed to know the customs within his realm, and therefore his law is thought to abrogate all contrary customs without mentioning them.

The enactment of Pope Boniface does not speak of immemorial customs, and therefore does not require express mention for their abrogation. But commentators [120] have inferred that an immemorial custom is not abrogated unless: (a) The law declares all contrary

[119] Suarez, *de leg.*, L. VII, c. 20, n. 5.

[120] Bauduin, *De consuet.*, nn. 216-218; Suarez, *de leg.*, L. VII, c. 20, n. 17.

customs abolished; (b) a reason is expressed in the law against an immemorial custom; (c) the law abrogates every custom, even those which it leaves undesignated.[121] It has been said that the "possession of time immemorial is, as it were, a title, the best possible title . . . Moreover a very old custom, or one exceeding the memory of men, has the force of privilege conceded by the ruler."[122] Even a particular law must mention such a custom, if it is to be abrogated.[123]

(c) By revocatory clause. When a legislator adds a revocatory clause, the phrase is to be weighed carefully. If he chooses a phrase which condemns a contrary custom as irrational, a corruption of law, he takes the very foundation from the custom, even if it be immemorial. But such a clause is rather reprobatory than revocatory. Whether such a condemnation kills the custom beyond resurrection has been explained under the study of reasonableness.[124] If the clause revokes a custom without calling it unreasonable, then the law speaks only of the past.[125] The most common clause "*non obstante consuetudine contraria*" revokes only general contrary customs.[126] When the word "*quacumque*" or "*nulla*" are added the clause also affects particular customs, according to Reiffenstuel.[127] If the legislator uses a phrase which indicates that he revokes all customs "except this or that one," his meaning is clear and is to be taken literally.[128]

Article 10. The Proof of Custom

When the doctrine had become clearer that the legal essence of custom is the consent of the ruler given to the factual custom of the people, the question of proof becomes a secondary matter. The burden of proof, if it is necessary, rests on the one who invokes it.

[121] Bouix, *Tract. de prin.*, p. 395.

[122] Reiffenstuel, lib. I, tit. IV, n. 189.

[123] Bauduin, *De consuet.*, n. 214.

[124] *Cf. supra* 61.

[125] Suarez, *de leg.*, L. VII, c. 7, n. 3; Reiffenstuel, lib. I, tit. IV, n. 186.

[126] Zallinger, lib. I, tit. IV, § 239, III. Wernz, however, thinks this revokes particular customs, not privileged—*Jus Decretalium*, I, n. 193, II.

[127] Reiffenstuel, lib. I, tit. IV, n. 183.

[128] Reiffenstuel, lib. I, tit. IV, n. 192.

He may attempt this in two ways through witnesses or through judicial sentences.

Two witnesses affirming that a major part of a community has observed a custom for the required time give full proof; if it be an immemorial custom full proof will be had if the witnesses assert that they have always heard from their elders that such has been the uncontradicted custom.[129] A custom notoriously public needs no proof.[130] Written proof is acceptable, if perchance the custom has been reduced to script. Van Espen thinks that proof by witnesses is more valuable than documentary proof, that, in fact, written proof is of no value in some cases.[131]

A custom may be proved also by judicial sentences. It has been shown that a court decision is not necessary to introduce a custom.[132] A judgment in favor of custom over the law is not needed, but for utility's sake, it is desired.[133] A judgment then is a great help in proving custom.[134]

It has been said, however, that no proof is needed because custom is law and needs no proof.[135] Yet, although custom is a law, it is also a fact, which needs to be proved unless it be already notorious. Because the consent of the ruler is primary, the question of proof has been studied very little in the matter of custom. Even as thorough a writer as Suarez has not much to say about proof. And this is natural, it seems, because custom for the most part will follow the ordinary procedure of proof in other matters.

[129] Bauduin, *De consuet.*, n. 201.

[130] Reiffenstuel, lib. I, tit. IV, n. 180.

[131] Van Espen, *Jus eccles. univ.*, Pars III, tit. 7, c. 6.

[132] Suarez, *de leg.*, L. VII, c. 11, n. 4.

[133] Schmalzgrueber, lib. I, tit. IV, n. 17.

[134] Bouix, *Tract de prin.*, p. 352; Reiffenstuel, lib. I, tit. IV, n. 176; Suarez, *de leg.*, L. VII, c. 11, n. 10.

[135] Puchta, *Das Gewohnheitsrecht*, I, n. 104ff.; II, p. 165ff.

Part II

COMMENTARY ON THE LEGISLATION OF THE CODE

CHAPTER VI

COMMENTARY ON THE LEGISLATION OF THE CODE

Article 1. The Bridge Between the Old and the New Law

Canon 5. Vigentes in praesens contra horum statuta canonum consuetudines sive universales sive particulares, si quidem ipsis canonibus expresse *reprobentur*, tamquam iuris corruptelae corrigantur, licet sint immemorabiles, neve sinantur in posterum reviviscere; aliae, quae quidem centenariae sint et immemorabiles, tolerari poterunt, si ordinarii pro locorum ac personarum adiunctis existiment eas prudenter submoveri non posse; ceterae suppressae habeantur, nisi expresse codex aliud caveat.

When the new Code of Canon Law was beginning to take form, canonists waited with no little expectation to learn what the legislator would do concerning the many customs that had grown up during the legal disorder which necessitated the codification. The mind of the legislator, it seemed, would be to reorder the whole legal system.[1] A rigorous defense was forecast in the new law's attitude towards custom. It was anticipated that no custom would be tolerated either beside the law or against the law, until it had attained the ripe age of one hundred years or until its origin had passed out of the memory of men. When the Code appeared Canon 5 expressed the attitude of the legislator towards all custom which antedated the codification. This transitional canon did not abolish future customs; it brought order out of chaos and left the way open for new customs to be established according to the principles of the second title in the first book of the Code.

[1] Wernz, *Jus Decretalium,* I, n. 194, II, 190, IV.

A. Customs Against the New Law

(a) Customs expressly reprobated.

In Canon 5 the new law bridges the present and the past in this way. Some customs of the past are *expressly reprobated* and must be corrected. They are to be considered as corruptions of law. Even customs of the longest duration, customs immemorial and centenary, must be abolished if they are reprobated. The words *"neve sinantur in posterum reviviscere"* have provoked various interpretations. The opinion is offered that such customs can never again be resurrected. They are declared forever unreasonable.[2] Michiels seems to say that this reprobation does not outlaw the custom forever, but that it constitutes a prohibitory clause. The reprobated custom then, which existed before the Code, can become law after the Code, only through the temporal duration that is centenary or immemorial. (Canon 27, § 1).[3] Whether or not a custom once reprobated can ever revive will be considered under Canon 27, § 2, where the question of reasonableness is treated more completely.[4]

(b) Customs not expressly reprobated.

There are many other customs which are against the law, but which the Canons fail to condemn expressly. What force have these? It may be said apodictically that every custom opposed to the new Code must be suppressed. But there is a certain provision made for those customs which have attained centenary or immemorial age.

1. Centenary and Immemorial Customs.

If at the time the Code went into effect there existed a custom one hundred years old and immemorial the local Ordinary may tolerate it, if he foresees that the custom cannot be prudently removed. It might be asked if there is any difference between a centenary custom and an immemorial custom. The word *"et"* in the text of the law would seem to indicate a difference. It cannot be said that "immemorial" designates of necessity a longer time than one hundred years. Such an opinion would assume the age of the modern human to be one hundred years. Therefore, according to this theory, im-

[2] Maroto, *Inst.*, I, n. 170; Augustine, *Commentary,* I, nn. 76 and 111.

[3] Michiels, *Normae Generales,* I, 78; *cf. infra* 119.

[4] *Cf. infra* 106.

memorial means customs beyond one hundred years.[5] The preferable opinion is that even a custom one hundred years old may not be immemorial, and yet not every immemorial custom must be at least one hundred years old. The term "immemorial" does not mean that the time of the custom's beginning is unknown or that proof of its age cannot be established. It rather means that nothing contrary to the practice has been done, said or heard within the memory of the living. Such a custom may be either longer or shorter than one hundred years.[6] It may be concluded then that there is a difference between the terms *centenariae* and *immemorabiles.* The latter may be realized by some eighty or ninety years.[7] In the Code, however, the two customs are generally treated as equal,[8] unless the law demands exactly one hundred years.[9]

It is said that these privileged customs are left to the prudence of the Ordinary (Canon 198, § 1). But the Ordinary may not retain or abolish these according to his own whim. Any custom against the universal law is outside the province of the Ordinary. The position of the Ordinary is well shown in a response of the Sacred Congregation of the Council. A custom had existed for one hundred years, whereby an archbishop appointed assistants without consulting the pastors. Before the Code the appointment of assistants was not done in a uniform way. The custom is now contrary to the Code but it is not expressly reprobated. Since the custom in question was centenary the Ordinary, according to Canon 5, might tolerate it, if in his prudence he feared greater evils from its abolition. But the very fact that the Ordinary asked the question seemed to indicate that there was a possibility of correcting the custom. The reply was given that Canon 476, § 3 is to be observed.[10] Another diocese had a custom whereby pewholders in dispute with the bishop appealed against him to the civil courts. The bishop, to avoid attract-

[5] Vermeersch-Creusen, *Epitome,* I, n. 142, deny that an immemorial custom must be older than a centenary custom.

[6] Benedict XIV, const. *Inter multa,* April 4, 1747—*Fontes* 379.

[7] Augustine, *Comment.,* I, 112; Cocchi, *Comment.,* I, n. 89.

[8] *Cf.* Canons 27, 30, 63, § 2.

[9] *Cf.* Canons 1511, § 1; 102, § 1.

[10] *Cf.* S. C. C. *Resolutio,* 13 Nov., 1920—*AAS,* XIII (1921), 43-46.

ing odium upon ecclesiastical authority, desired to continue the practice. The Sacred Congregation of the Council replied that when the parties freely come before the Ordinary, they should not be referred to the lay tribunal, and efforts should be made to remove the practice of appealing to the civil courts.[11] This makes it clear that a bishop must make every effort to abolish even these privileged customs.[12] When there are questions pertaining to his administration, it should be easy to abolish the custom. And any rate, it is beyond the power of the Ordinary to give such customs legal status. His toleration is only a negative act. If change of circumstances makes it prudent, the Ordinary must abolish the custom.[13]

2. Customs Not Centenary or Immemorable.

Those custom which are against the law and which have not attained privileged age are to be considered suppressed. The Canon adds, however, "unless the Code expressly ordains otherwise." Thus throughout the Code are various laws which, as it were, canonize some customs with the words *salvis legitimis consuetudinibus, salva contraria consuetudine, nisi aliter consuetudinibus fuerit constitutum, nisi obstet consuetudo, excepto casu consuetudinis*.[14] It may be concluded then that all customs contrary to the new Code are suppressed. Some may be tolerated but they are not legalized.

[11] *Cf.* S. C. C. *Resolutio,* 11 Dec., 1920—*AAS,* XIII (1921), 262-268.

[12] Canons 1291, 1438, however, mention *immemorabilis consuetudo* and give such customs the force of particular law.

[13] Van Hove, *Normae Generales,* n. 53, against Toso, *Comment. min.*, I, 18, and Vermeersch-Creusen, *Epitome,* I, n. 75.

[14] *Cf.* Canons 161, 168, 418, § 1; 422, § 2; 471, § 2; 1182, §§ 1 and 2; 1186, 1236, § 1; 1248, 1291, 1438, 1481. Canons 136, § 1; 1262, § 1, speak of the "*mores.*" Canons 161 and 1236, § 1, speak of the *jus particulare.* This includes customs.

An interesting point may be noted in n. 4 of the decrees and acts of an Irish Plenary Council held after the Code. It reads:

Consuetudines quaelibet Codicis praescriptis vel Decretis huius Concilii contrariae, nec eiusdem Codicis canonibus reprobatae, si centenariae sint aut immemorabiles, tolerari poterunt, modo Ordinarii pro locorum ac personarum adiunctis existiment eas prudenter submoveri non posse; ceterae autem suppressae habeantur, nisi Codex VEL HAEC SYNODUS aliud expresse caveat.—*Acta et Decreta Concilii Plenarii Episcoporum Hiberniae apud Maynutiam,* August 2-15, 1927. The capitals in the text are the writer's.

B. Custom Beside the New Law

Canon 5 provides for custom against the law, but what is to be said of custom which flourished beside the law at the time of the codification? Canon 5 is silent. It seems evident that *particular* customs beside the law remain in force. The Code, in a word, is not particularly concerned about customs beside the law. The main concern of the new legislator was to abolish countless customs contrary to the discipline of the codification. He retains particular customs *praeter legem* even as he has not abolished particular laws.

It is not so evident, however, concerning *universal* customs beside the law. The opinion is expressed that these customs are abrogated by Canon 5.[15] Another doctrine is advanced that such universal customs can remain as particular customs, particular law.[16] For several reasons, however, it seems necessary to hold that even universal customs beside the law are not abolished by Canon 5. First of all the silence of Canon 5 seems to exclude even universal customs. Although it may be admitted that the mind of the codification was to effect a certain unity in the law, it does not follow that the legislator of necessity wished to abolish all universal customs beside the law. His enactment of Canon 5 shows that he considers this unity sufficiently effected by the abrogation of customs against the law. Indeed since he even tolerates certain privileged customs against the law can it be said that he abrogates universal customs *praeter legem* by mere silence? It has been objected that Canon 6, 6°, abrogates all universal laws even *praeter jus* which are not explicitly or implicitly contained in the Code and that therefore it includes universal customs. It seems gratuitous, however, to apply Canon 6 to custom. Clearly that canon concerns the written law, while Canon 5 provides for customary law. Finally if Canon 6, 6°, must be applied it is difficult to see how a universal custom *praeter legem* could be kept even as a particular law. The wording of the canon clearly abrogates absolutely universal laws not explicitly or implicitly contained in the Code. It can be concluded for these reasons that if a

[15] Maroto, *Inst.*, I, 170.

[16] Cappello, *Summa*, I, n. 55.

universal custom existed beside the Code, it is not abolished by Canon 5.[17]

It should be admitted that Canon 6, 5°, abolishes any general penal customs which might have arisen before the Code.

ARTICLE 2. *Titulus II De Consuetudine*

The first title of the first book in the Code deals with the written law. Quite naturally then the second title follows with some principles concerning the unwritten law, or custom. The second title in no way intends to exhaust the canonical concept of custom. One looks in vain for even a definition of custom, nor will one find the expression *jus consuetudinarium* in the codification.[18] Not without reason does the historical section of this work represent half its pages. It will be seen that the Code has left many juridical points and practical topics of consideration intimately connected with the question of custom to the teaching of canonists.

The word *consuetudo* is derived from the Latin *consuesco, consuefacere, frequenter facere* and more remotely from the Greek ἦθος ἔθος.[19] The word is found in various canons of the Code. It may be translated generally by the English word "custom." But it does not always have the same general significance, for, besides its legal meaning, it may also bear a non-legal signification.

In its non-legal meaning the word designates merely the fact that there is uniformity of action in a certain matter. This is often called a custom of fact (*consuetudo facti*). There are several canons in which *consuetudo* signifies the uniformity, the custom of fact, which precedes the introduction of any legal obligation.[20]

In other canons, however,—and this is of more concern,—*consuetudo* means a law, a legal obligation. This real juridical obligation is called a custom of law (*consuetudo legis*). In this usage it means that the acts of the people, the custom of fact, have produced a real law, because they have realized the conditions demanded by

[17] Vermeersch-Creusen, *Epitome*, n. 75; Cicognani, *Jus can.*, II, 34.

[18] Wehrle, *De la coutume*, p. 408.

[19] Forcellini, *Lexicon totius latinitatis*, v. "*consuetudo.*"

[20] *Cf.* Canons 27, § 1; 28, 63, § 1; 134, 1131, § 2; 1555, § 1; 1613, § 1; 1805, 2024, 2080.

the legislator.[21] Sometimes the legislator shows even more definitely the obligatory meaning of *consuetudo* by appending certain adjectives. The legislation concerning episcopal visitation (Canon 346), fast and abstinence (Canon 1251, § 1), the privileges of patrons (Canon 1455, 3°), the law of tithes and first fruits (Canon 1502), the cathedraticum (Canon 1504), the question of donation of church property (Canon 1535)—all take cognizance of customs called *legitima, probata, laudabilis, antiqua.*

Although the Code uses the word *consuetudo* to mean a legal obligation, it does not give a definition of custom. This is left to the common doctrine of canonists. The concise notion of custom will be demonstrated after each of its elements has been studied in the consequent chapters. But here it will be well to assemble certain kindred notions, which have been treated throughout the historical section in various places, notions which at times may be confused with custom.

In the Code is found the word *mores.* The laws concerning liturgical rite (Canon 98, § 5), the clerical tonsure (Canon 136, § 1), the age for licit marriage (Canon 1067, § 2), the proper head-dress in church (Canon 1262, § 2), all take notice of the *mores* of a place. This word signifies rather an accustomed way of acting, not a legal obligation as understood by the word *consuetudo.* But in Canons 762 and 793 *mos* has the connotation of customary law.

In its legislation concerning the computing of time (Canon 33, § 1), sacred images (Canon 1279, § 2), processions (Canon 1295), taxes (Canon 1833, 2°) and court citations (Canon 1877),—the Code pays deference to the *usus* of a place. This term likewise does not signify a legal obligation.

Consuetudo, even in its legal meaning, does not connote the same thing as *lex. Lex* means rather that legal obligation which originates entirely and exclusively in the will of the legislator. The legislator may promulgate his will orally or in writing (Canon 9). And even when his will is expressed orally, although it may have the appearance of custom, such an enactment differs essentially from custom, which originates in the will of the people. The oral will of the legislator is *lex.*

[21] *Cf.* Canons 5, 25, 26, 30.

Nor is custom to be confused with ***tradition.*** Tradition in its legal acceptation is that whole body of laws which has been handed down. It may embrace not only custom, but also the enactments of a legislator. Perhaps the occasion of the laws' promulgation has long since been forgotten, yet they are *leges*, not *consuetudines*. The term tradition, then, has a wider scope than custom.[22]

As has been noted in the historical pages of this work, ***prescription*** and custom were long confused. Yet they have nothing in common but use and time. Prescription gives a subjective right to private individuals. It requires both good faith and a title. Custom creates an objective law. It is produced by a community, with the consent of the legislator. Neither a title nor good faith are necessary. But if a situation implies a subjective right along with an objective norm, if the rights of a private person are involved, custom is said to be mixed with prescription, and its temporal duration is to be ruled accordingly.[23]

The term ***observance*** is sometimes used. Observance is either the repetition or the continued omission of acts, in as much as it is considered either negatively or positively. It is like custom in as much as it consists of usage or practice. It differs, however, from custom in many respects. No fixed time is required to establish observance, while custom must be prescribed. Observance may be the product of a physical person as well as that of a community. It is enough that acts be repeated more or less frequently to establish observance. It may be considered either as a fact or as a law. As a fact, it is the repetition of acts concerning the same matters; as a law, it is the law which results from that fact. Observance then, while it may at times designate a custom of fact, acts not yet clothed with the necessary conditions to become law, differs in many respects from customary law. Some apply the word observance to the ***stylus curiae.***

The ***stylus curiae*** is spoken of in the suppletory law of Canon 20 and in Canon 42, § 1. The term ***stylus*** comes from the blunt instrument once used in scratching words on wax. From this usage, the word was applied to the sentence of the court and then it came to

[22] *Cf. supra* 4 note; Cappello, *Summa*, I, n. 108; Wernz, *Jus Decretalium*, I, n. 185, I.

[23] *Cf. infra* 118.

mean the usual mode in which a definite court acted. It is also known as the *praxis curiae* which is the mode of procedure followed by a court in expediting causes and other matters. The term *curia* applies to both the Roman Curia and the Diocesan Curia. Each dicastery has its own mode of procedure. This *stylus,* as it is called, is sometimes referred to as the custom of the Curia. So Canon 1555, § 1, says the Holy Office retains its *propriam consuetudinem. Stylus* may be considered as a fact or as a law. As a fact it means only usage; as a law, it signifies rules and laws which result from that fact. It might be well to show by an example how the custom of the court arises. It was a moot question before the Code whether a bishop could use his faculties for dispensing, when there was a (cumulatio facultatum) need to combine his powers in one and the same case. The canonists were divided upon the question. But the custom of the Sacred Congregations did not allow the use of cumulation unless there was given an express permission in the faculties. Canon 1049 finally settled the dispute, but before this legislation the *stylus* had governed the norm of action. *Stylus* then is not custom, but only the fact of similarity of action by a court. *Stylus* is the product of *lex, usus, observantia,* and all those elements which influence judges.

Another notion in some way akin to custom is *jurisprudence,* when it is taken to mean the practice of judges or tribunals. It is the *stylus* which has acquired firm and fixed characteristics. After an adequate number of uniform decisions and a lapse of time jurisprudence may become obligatory. An individual judgment rendered in a case does not obtain force of law for all.[24] Even the decisions of the Rota are particular for the parties themselves. It may be admitted, however, that jurisprudence of a court can create a custom for that body itself, provided the conditions needed for custom are realized.[25] Jurisprudence differs from the *stylus* in that the latter is not always obligatory outside the Roman Curia, for example, whereas the former influence the procedure of the lower courts.[26]

[24] Data per modum sententiae iudicialis . . . vim legis non habet, et ligat tantum personas (Canon 17, § 3). Facit ius inter partes . . . (Canon 1904, § 2).

[25] Michiels, *Normae Generales,* II, 45.

[26] Cicognani, *Jus can.,* I, 122; Michiels, *Normae Generales,* II, 44; Vermeersch-Creusen, *Epitome,* I, n. 127.

Finally the ***opinion of doctors*** of Canon Law does not create a custom. It does form a suppletory source of law.[27] The opinions of doctors, however, may be the font by which a community begins to introduce custom. But of themselves canonists are not legislators and they cannot make either law or custom.[28]

Article 3. The Legal Essence of Custom, the Consent of the Legislator

Canon 25. Consuetudo in ecclesia vim legis a consensu competentis superioris ecclesiastici unice obtinet.

A. Why a Superior's Consent is Needed

The first canon of this title immediately affirms the essential element of custom, viewed as a law. It establishes the place of custom in the Church which is different from civil juridical societies. For in the hierarchical monarchy of the Church the people have no legislative power.[29] Although the laity may have begun a practice and established a custom of fact, there is still not even the semblance of a law, since it is only the consent of the superior which gives a legal stamp to a practice of the people. Even this consent does not delegate a legal power to the people. It is rather an approval given by the ecclesiastical superior to the acts of the people.[30] To say that custom has its legal force only from the consent of the superior is not to deny the part of the people in its formation. It will be shown later that custom always originates with the people, not with the legislator.

B. Ways in Which Superior May Consent

The superior may consent to a custom in several ways. The Code itself is silent concerning the manner in which consent may be given. The general doctrine of the canonists is to be considered. A superior

[27] Si . . . desit expressum praescriptum legis . . . norma sumenda est . . . a communi constantique sententia doctorum (Canon 20).

[28] Michiels, *Normae Generales,* II, 44.

[29] Benedict XIV, *De Syn. dioecesana,* lib. XII, c. 8, n. 8; lib. IX, c. 1, n. 6; Pius VI, cons. *Auctorem fidei,* Aug. 28, 1794—*Fontes,* n. 476. Pius X, ency. *Vehementer nos,* Feb. 11, 1906—*Fontes,* n. 671.

[30] *Cf.* Canons 218, § 1, and 329, § 1.

may approve of custom in a SPECIAL way. To give such consent it is necessary that the superior know a custom, because *nil volitum nisi praecognitum.* The ruler may give this special consent in two ways, expressly or tacitly. When he uses words or signs to express his approval he is said to give special *expressed* consent. When the silence of the legislator is such that it indicates consent, he is considered to have given special *tacit* consent.[31] This latter consent of course must be real, not a silence provoked for example by fear of schism or dictated by prudence because of civil powers. This consent is based on the rule of law which says *qui tacet, consentire videtur.*[32]

There is a second kind of consent which is intimated in Canons 27 and 28. This consent is called LEGAL. It is given in this way. The legislator places certain conditions beforehand. He then says in effect that he will approve any custom which measures up to these conditions. It was already the common doctrine before the Code that such legal consent suffices. In such a situation it is not necessary that the ruler know every custom. He does know it, as it were, in general, through antecedent conditions. He speaks his approval through the law. It is after all fitting that there be such a consent to remove from the conscience of men the obligation of a less useful law or to approve a custom which, supplying law, produces unity. It is certain that legal consent suffices.[33]

C. *The Superior Competent to Give Consent*

1. For *legal consent* provision is made in Canons 27 and 28. When a superior has given legal approval, the subordinate cannot

[31] Some writers call this interpretative consent—Cappello, *Summa,* I, p. 94, note 6. Others speak of presumed consent—Toso, *Comment. min.,* I, 81.

[32] R. J. 43 in VI°; S. C. C. (no date given)—*AAS,* XX (1928), 146. Catholics having recourse to civil powers cannot bring about a custom against the *privilegium fori* in the United States. *Cf. infra* 100, where this case is considered.

[33] J. Kinane, "The nature of the consent on the part of a superior necessary for custom," *The Irish Ecclesiastical Record,* XXXVI (1930), 646; Ojetti, *Comment.,* I, 172; Michiels, *Normae Generales,* II, 34; Cicognani, *Jus can.,* II, 158; Van Hove, *De consuet.,* n. 68; Toso, *Comment., min.,* I, 81; Trummer, *Die Gewohnheit als kirckliche Rechtsquelle,* p. 25.

refuse his approval in his territory. The Code itself grants this consent to customs, which can qualify, and no lesser legislator can oppose the common law. Indeed, if the custom has already measured up to the legal conditions stated by the superior, it has already received his approval and is law. This can be attacked only by the enactment of a contrary law (Canon 30). An inferior, however, might attack indirectly a custom in the course of formation, by not allowing it to realize necessary conditions. He may reprobate it and call it unreasonable within his own territory. He may thus interrupt the temporal duration which it requires.[34] Indeed it is even the bishop's duty to safeguard the law of the Code. He can, however, make his own judgment whether he should favor in his locality a custom against the universal law, or prevent its realization by condemning the practice before it becomes a law. For example, a bishop might think that in his compact, well populated diocese there is no reason for celebrating Mass without some server, or he might conclude that in certain places, on certain missions it is extremely difficult for a priest to obtain a server. The inferior legislator, therefore, must form his own decision concerning a custom against the law of a superior. If he chooses to condemn, or even to punish the transgressor of the universal law, he must do so in some public manner. If, in his prudence, he thinks there is cause for acting against the Code, he may maintain silence.

2. Concerning the *special consent* of the superior competent to approve custom there is need of a distinction. A custom which receives special consent refers either to the universal law or to particular law. (a) Customs which refer to the *universal law* and which are *against* the common law need the consent of the Sovereign Pontiff, if they are to receive special approval. This applies to all customs which seek special consent against that law, whether these customs be general or particular. On the other hand customs which are *beside* the universal law are either general or particular. If general, they need the approval of the Pope. But if they are particular, not universal, there is need only of the consent of that superior who has legislative power over those who introduce the custom. (b) Customs

[34] Trummer, *Die Gewohnheit*, p. 29; Michiels, *Normae Generales*, II, 38.

which refer to ***particular law*** are likewise either against the law or beside it. If they be ***against*** the law, the author of that law must give consent. A bishop, for example, can approve custom against synodal enactments; he cannot, however, approve custom against provincial law. The metropolitan can do nothing concerning customs in suffragan Sees, since he has no legislative power there. If, however, the custom be ***beside*** the particular law, it suffices that the superior of the community introducing custom gives consent.

D. Custom Has Force of Law

The Code says that custom obtains the force of law. The civil law systems in no way give custom the place it enjoins in Canon Law. Civil lawyers, therefore, at times raise the question if there really is such a thing as custom with force of law. When a ruler gives consent does he not equivalently edit a statute law? [35] It is maintained by canonists that custom is law essentially and only because of the legislator's consent. It seems then to the civilists, in particular when they consider the notion of special consent, that the ruler really edits a law. What then is the difference between custom and statute law?

It may be admitted first of all that if a legislator gives his consent to a custom and intends to reëdit it as law, it ceases to be a custom and becomes law. The opinion of Suarez [36] that the bond of custom still remains, together with the bond of law, seems untenable. Rather the legislator withdraws his consent from the custom and expresses it in (***lex***) law.[37] This has happened to many customs in the course of time. They have been codified. Then they are no longer customary law. But when a ruler approves a custom without intending to reëdit it as law, there remains an essential difference between ***consuetudo*** and the ***lex***. A custom always originates with the people, not with the ruler. A law is always promulgated, at least orally (Canon 9). There is no promulgation for custom. Nevertheless, there are some canonists, who agree with the civilists, that at least with special consent there can hardly be an obligation induced by

[35] Benedict XIV, const. *Singulari*, Feb. 9, 1749, § 10—*Fontes*, n. 394.

[36] *Cf. supra* 45, Suarez, *de leg.*, L. VII, c. 2, n. 4.

[37] Michiels, *Normae Generales*, II, 8; Ojetti, *Comment.*, I, 168.

way of custom. They affirm that the only essential difference between custom and law is the promulgation. The fact that the title of the Code, which deals with custom, does not explicitly speak of special consent might indicate with this opinion that the legislator no longer admits that a real custom is introduced by special consent. This opinion would, therefore, consider special consent as a source of law, not of custom.[38] It seems, however, that there is room for the doctrine of special consent, as already explained,[39] although it may be admitted that it is more difficult to distinguish *lex* from a custom introduced with special *expressed* consent than when the consent is *legal.*

Although it is said that custom has the force of law and is the same as statute law in its binding power, it is readily admitted that a system of customary law alone would not be workable. Customary law is not so uniform nor so certain as statute law. And this is also why the logic of the Code of Canon Law deals in the first title with written law and then only in the second title introduces a secondary source of rights and obligations whereby the first is interpreted, supplemented and at times abolished.

Long is the list of canons, which show respect for established customs. Many are the laws which canonize certain customs. Each case must be studied to know if the word *consuetudo* refers to a custom of fact or to a custom of law. Even though the terminology in a certain canon may refer to a mere custom of fact which has not yet obtained the force of law, still the received usage must be obeyed. The obedience which is tendered is due not because of the acknowledged existence of a customary law, but because the written law has embodied the practice or usage as a part of its legislation. Thus the *mores,* the *usus* and the *consuetudo facti* will have legal force, not as customary law, but by reason of the canon which mentions them.[40] The legislation of the Code which takes cognizance of custom is very extensive. Recognition of custom is found, for example, in the law concerning rescripts, even when conceded *motu*

[38] Vermeersch-Creusen, *Epitome,* I, n. 139; Wehrle, *De la coutume,* p. 408, doubts the actual existence of customary law.

[39] *Cf. supra* 83; Michiels, *Normae Generales,* II, 34.

[40] Van Hove, *De consuet.,* p. 12, note 1. *Cf. supra* 79.

proprio (Canon 46), the canon concerning privileges (Canon 63), the rules of precedence (Canon 106, 5°, 6°), the prescriptions relative to proper clerical garb (Canon 136, § 1), the regulations for convoking an election (Canon 162, § 1), the norm to be followed when the sick and infirm cast a written ballot (Canon 168), the legal enactments governing the episcopal visitation (Canon 346), the precedence in chapters (Canon 408, § 1), the giving of a stipend to a capitular substitute celebrant (Canon 417, § 2), the support accorded to a canon or a capitular emeritus (Canon 422, § 2), the salary of the vicar capitular (Canon 441, 1°), the blessing of homes on Holy Saturday (Canon 462, 6°), the perquisites of the pastor (Canon 463, § 1), the appointment of parochial vicars (Canon 471, §§ 2, 4), the residence of curates in the territory of the parish to which they are assigned (Canon 476, § 5), the dowry (Canon 547, § 1), the minister of baptism in territories where parishes or quasi-parishes do not exist (Canon 740), the employment of a god-parent at baptism (Canon 762, § 1), the use of a sponsor at confirmation (Canon 793), the amount of the manual Mass-stipend, if no definite sum has been determined by the local Ordinary (Canon 831, § 2), the ringing of church bells for profane purposes (Canon 1169, § 4), the celebration of divine services and ecclesiastical rites in dedicated churches or oratories (Canon 1171), the right of a church to use the title of a basilica (Canon 1180), the pastor's administration of church offerings (Canon 1182, §§ 1, 2), the appointment and dismissal of sextons and other like functionaries employed in the service of the church (Canon 1185), the making of repairs in cathedral, parochial and non-parochial churches (Canon 1186), the indexes of funeral fees (Canon 1234, § 1), the question of public mercantile dealings on Sundays and Holydays (Canon 1248), the obligation of fast and abstinence (Canon 1251, § 1), the fixing of days for the holding of processions (Canon 1290, § 2), the solemn celebration of the Corpus Christi procession (Canon 1291, § 1), the observance of the regularly appointed processions (Canon 1294, § 1), the support of benefices and the accrual of the *jura stolae* (Canon 1410), the lifetime conferment of secular benefices (Canon 1438), the canonical installation of pastors in office (Canon 1444, § 1), the privileges attached to ecclesiastical advowson (Canon 1455, 3°), the making of uncommon or unusual repairs in the residential abode of beneficed clerics (Canon 1477, § 2), the appointment of the annual revenues yielding from a benefice to its diverse incumbents (Canon 1480), the distribution of these same revenues during a term of vacancy (Canon 1481), the consignment of tithes and first fruits (Canon 1502), the tendering of the cathedraticum (Canon 1504), the administration of church goods (Canon 1519, § 2), the administrative capacities of the Council of Finance (Canon 1520, § 1), the bestowal of moderate donations drawn from the movable goods of the church (Canon 1535), the serving of judicial processes (Canon 1591). It is evident, therefore, that custom is an influential factor in the ulimate constitution and application of law. Although not the equivalent of statute, custom, nevertheless, plays an important rôle in Canon Law.

E. *The Doctrine of the "Opinio Juris"*

Custom might be said to be composed of two essential elements. A custom of fact begins with the acts of a community and to this a legislator gives consent and thus effects a custom of law. It has just been established [41] that the *legal essence* of custom must be placed in an ecclesiastical legislator. The protagonists of the doctrine called *Opinio Juris,* however, place the essence of custom in a kind of common persuasion of the people. This teaching was first received into the civil law school of thought.[42] It was Schulte who tried to apply the doctrine of the *Opinio Juris* to Canon Law. His doctrine might be outlined in this way. The books of the Decretals, which are the sole official doctrine at this time, do not give a treatise on customary law, although they may solve certain difficulties concerning such law. All law, this doctrine continues, flows from two fonts, namely, from a legislator or from the people. The will of the legislator can enact laws, but it is certain that his laws do not cover every possible situation. And in this contingency, the will of the people becomes a source of law. But this doctrine departs from the accepted notion of custom, which originates with the people, by placing the essence of custom

[41] *Cf. supra* 82.

[42] *Cf.* Friedrich Karl von Savigny, *System de heutigen romischen Rechts,* I, Berlin, 1840; Puchta, *Das Gewohnheitsrecht,* Erlangen, 1828-1837.

in a common juridical persuasion that something is a law. When the majority of people adopt a practice, their usage indicates and manifests the common persuasion, just as a written enactment shows the will of the legislator. This second source of law, the popular persuasion, can be limited and subjected by the legislative font of law to the fulfillment of certain specified conditions. But as long as the legislator has not placed any conditions, as long as he has set up no restrictions whatsoever, then the common persuasion manifested in the actions of the people will achieve in its own right the force of law for their consistent practice.[43]

This doctrine which is directly opposed by Canon 25, is clearly unsound and hardly any canonist would sustain it today. It will be shown elsewhere that custom is founded in the will of a community, rather than in the juridical persuasion of the popular intellect. It is clear that the vast body of the faithful in the Church are not legislators, as this teaching implies. Popular action begins a custom, but such is the constitution of the Church, that the legal element can come only from an ecclesiastical legislator.

Scholion—Custom and Faculties

A privilege might be defined as a private law concerning a favor which dispenses the privileged person from obedience to some law or which gives him powers beyond those fixed by the ordinary provisions of law. Certain special privileges are called faculties. The most widely known perhaps are the *Facultates Quinquennales,* which are given to Ordinaries when they make their report to the Consistorial Congregation.

Bishops often communicate these faculties, at least in part, to their priests. Through this usage a diocese, for example, after a period of time develops a practice. The question arises, therefore, whether the use of such faculties over a prescribed time can create a custom.

In the answer to this general question will be found the response to a particular problem, which is most practical. Many Ordinaries once communicated to priests the faculty to say Mass without a server. In the course of time this faculty was revoked. Canon 813

[43] Schulte, *Das katholische Kirchenrecht,* I, 209-214.

now says that a priest shall not celebrate Mass without a minister who serves and answers him. It may be admitted that this obligation is *per se* grievous. But the question may be asked whether custom does not excuse from the law. Let it be presumed that the custom is centenary or immemorial, for if it were not, it would be suppressed according to Canon 5. Let it be supposed that the custom cannot be prudently removed. It does not change the question to say that the faculty contained a clause *"si necessitas urgeat"* since it was out of necessity that the practice developed. Let it be admitted that the faculty was used properly and granting this, can it be said that a custom has been established, since it was by virtue of a faculty that the practice was formed? The answer to this problem concerning the Mass server may be found in a solution of the question whether a custom may grow simultaneously with the use of an indult.

Some attempt towards an affirmative answer might be made in in this way. An indult can be considered from two aspects. Some have in view more directly a release from the law while others are given more specifically to calm conscience. The faculty to dispense from the banns of marriage, for example, is given to be applied as a release from the law, when a canonical cause is present. A faculty, such as to say Mass without a server, is granted to ease scruples of individuals.

The following situation might be pictured. A practice begins in a certain diocese contrary to the law. In a few years it becomes the more popular usage, but it has not yet realized the juridical conditions needed to establish customary law. Because of the scruples of a certain number the bishop communicates the faculty which frees them from the common law. Along with the indult then the practice continues running its prescribed time. Can customary law be thus established?

Let is be further presumed that the majority who carry out a usage might be convinced that there is no need for a faculty. They are convinced that the common law itself should not bind under the particular circumstances. Since the community which forms the custom knows that the faculty can be withdrawn at any time, cannot those introducing the practice intend rather to abrogate the common law by custom?

In spite of these considerations, however, it seems that the development of a custom cannot run simultaneously with the presence of a faculty. There seems to be a contradiction in juridical terms to have a custom against a law, when the legislator has taken the law away for a particular situation. It is difficult to see how there would be an intention to abrogate a law, which for the individual community no longer is of obligation.

Furthermore, when a legislator revokes an indult his purpose is to bring the people back to an observance of the common law. If the practice were to continue as an established customary law, there would hardly be any purpose in revoking the faculty.

Those who uphold the doctrine that no intention is needed in the people who act against the law, may be able, unlike those who require intention, to avoid the first objection, but the question of the revocation of the faculty presents a barrier to both the one and the other.

Certainly it should be admitted, however, that the usage, or custom of fact, which perdured during the time of the indult lays an excellent foundation for the development of a new custom which may readily grow out of the former practice, and it may even leave many persons in good faith concerning their actions.

Scholion—Is Customary Law Personal?

The question presents itself whether those who enjoy a custom in one locality can carry that custom with them to another place. Can Europeans, for example, bring their customary law to the United States and maintain it here?

It may be noted that this question under consideration does not involve *peregrini,* but rather those who go from one place to another in order to establish a domicile in that place. Can a foreign group, then, disregard for example the law of abstinence on Friday, if it happens to be a feast day on which they were accustomed not to abstain in the old country?

It should be admitted that concerning this matter there seems to be no jurisprudence nor have any canonists been found who consider the question directly. It seems, however, that a conclusion can be reached from other principles of law not found in the second title of the first book of the Code.

Canonists have long applied the ordinary principles of the written law to customary law which concerns *peregrini*. Custom has always been considered territorial in its relation to *peregrini*. It would seem, therefore, at least by a parity of argument, that custom should be held territorial also for those who leave one place definitely in order to establish a domicile elsewhere.

The same indication might be found in a reply given to a question by the Sacred Congregation of the Council. It was asked: Are those on pilgrimage to Rome, by reason of a Jubilee, bound to observe the Roman custom which forbids milk products in the morning and evening of fast days, or may they follow the custom of their place of origin, which permits milk products? The reply given was: "In the audience of November 4, your petition for a dispensation from fast and abstinence in favor of pilgrims visiting Rome during the Holy Year was presented to the Holy Father. His Holiness has deigned to *dispense* them from the said laws for the time of the journey. With respect to *permitting* them to follow in Rome the practices and customs of their respective countries regarding food and fast, His Holiness declared that he is disposed to grant such an indult whenever the respective directors of pilgrimages make application for the same in writing."[44]

It is true that this reply refers to *peregrini*, but it indicates that transfer of local custom is not recognized. A dispensation was granted. Since *peregrini* cannot carry their customary law with them, by a stronger argument should not those domiciled in a particular place be subject to the discipline of the local Ordinary?

Furthermore since custom has the force of particular law, all the principles of particular laws should be applied to it. It is affirmed that there will hardly be a particular custom, therefore, which binds an *incola* or an *advena* outside the territory.[45]

Since custom and *lex* (*qua* law) are not essentially different and

[44] S. C. C., *Reply*, Nov. 15, 1924. *Cf.* Cicognani, *Jus can.*, II, 106, for Italian text.

[45] Vindex, *Domicilium et quasi-domicilium eorumque effectus in Codice iuris canonici*, Ius Pontificium, VI (1926), 112.

since the one is presumed territorial, it seems that the other should enjoy the same presumption.

It may be admitted that a custom referring to matter which in the common law is personal, should likewise be considered personal. A group of clerics, for example, can establish a personal custom concerning a personal obligation, such as the divine office.

It should readily be admitted also that when a people move from one locality to another, their practices easily place the foundation for the beginning of a new custom. Such people are often in good faith and if in the mind of the new legislator into whose territory they have come, the usage is reasonable, it may be prudent not to disturb their good faith.

Article 4. The People, The Originator of Custom

Canon 26. Communitas quae legis ecclesiasticae saltem recipiendae capax est potest consuetudinem inducere quam vim legis obtineat.

A. What Kind of Community?

A community which is at least capable of receiving an ecclesiastical law can introduce a custom which obtains the force of law. The word *saltem* might seem superfluous in the canon, but it has a double implication. First of all it recalls the old controversy which waged before Suarez, concerning the type of community which could introduce custom. When Suarez had made it clear that the people were only the proximate material cause of customary law and that the legal essence of custom was the consent of the ruler, it at the same time became evident that a community introducing custom need not be capable of *making* law, but only of *receiving* it. Secondly the word *saltem* implies the possibility of communities in the Church with legislative power. It is not impossible that communities, such as the chapter of a cathedral or collegiate church, enjoy legislative power.

B. What Communities?

After giving the general principle of the nature of the community, the Code is silent concerning what these communities may be. In its legislation concerning the clerical garb (Canon 136, § 1), certain episcopal expenses (Canon 346), fast and abstinence (Canon 1251, § 1), donation of Church property (Canon 1535) and the expenses incurred by the employment of experts and specialists as witnesses at a trial (Canon 1805), the Code speaks of *locorum consuetudines*, but nowhere is there found any direct statement concerning the communities which can introduce custom.

There remains after the Code a great divergence of opinion concerning this question. Authors set up a general principle of interpretation by a generic definition of the community which can introduce custom. They then proceed to enumerate the various specific communities which fit into their definitions. In an attempt to reduce the notion of a society capable of receiving ecclesiastical law to a concise principle, some authors have stressed the idea of a corporative community; other have placed the fundamental note in stability and perpetuity; while still others have emphasized perfection in rule and unity. And so it is said that any collegiate moral personality can introduce custom.[46] According to others there is required a certain autonomy.[47] Yet another looks for a relative degree of perfection in a society which introduces custom.[48] The corporative element is sought in a community by Augustine.[49] Finally there is an opinion which makes its definition of the *communitas legis ecclesiasticae recipiendae capax* so all-inclusive as to comprise any community to whose custom of fact the superior accords his consent.[50]

Perhaps the best attempt to find the fundamental element in a community capable of receiving law is that made by Van Hove.[51] Law has been defined as an *ordinatio rationis ad bonum commune*. More fundamental than perpetuity or stability is the element of law which looks to the common good. Since this is so, the search for the principle note of a community capable of receiving law should be directed to-

[46] Toso, *Comment. min.*, I, 84.

[47] Maroto, *Institutiones*, I, n. 252; Cappello, *Summa*, I, n. 112.

[48] Chelodi-Bertagnoli, *Ius de personis*, n. 72; A Coronata, *Institutiones*, I, n. 39.

[49] Augustine, *Commentary*, I, 109.

[50] Ojetti, *Comment.*, I, 175.

[51] Van Hove, *De consuet.*, n. 81.

wards a community over which presides a superior with a public office which looks towards the common good. Therefore, any juridicial relationship, which benefits the common good, not merely a private good, such as a family, may be a community capable of receiving law and, therefore, can induce custom.

From these various attempts at defining a community, which can receive law, come various opinions when canonists begin to specify what individual communities may induce custom. Since there are of necessity very many opinions, the best way towards the most acceptable teaching seems to be found in assembling the different doctrines into four groups. It will be clear that certain groups cannot introduce custom. It will be equally evident that certain other communities can begin customary law. Between these two classes will be found certain communities, which are doubtfully capable of producing custom.

1. It is evident that a custom *cannot* be introduced by a private person or by a family, for such are immediate subjects of precepts, not of laws.

2. It is generally agreed that a custom *can* be introduced by the Church universal, by a province, by a diocese, by a city. The Code itself seems to suppose customs in cathedral chapters and colleges and to grant them such a capacity.[52]

3. The consideration of what specific communities can *probably* bring about customary law will depend naturally upon how an individual canonist defines *cammunitas legis ecclesiasticae recipiendae capax*. The various definitions have been considered above.[53] Here it is only possible to enumerate by name the conclusions drawn by different canonists from their definitions. It is probable that a custom can be started by a parish.[54] Canons 1181 and 1290, § 2, seem to refer to legalized customs and, therefore, to support the opinion that parishes can introduce customary law.[55] Probably also a custom

[52] *Cf.* Canons 396, § 2; 403, 409, § 2; 418, § 1.

[53] *Cf. supra* 94.

[54] This is affirmed by Vermeersch-Creusen, *Epitome,* I, n. 138; Michiels, *Normae Generales,* II, 44 et I, 140-142; Kinane, "The community capable of introducing custom," *The Irish Ecclesiastical Record,* XXXVII (1931), 523, 524.

[55] However, Maroto, *Institutiones,* I, n. 252; Cocchi, *Comment.,* I, n. 135;

can be introduced by a deanery,[56] and by a college of clerics.[57] There is also a difference of opinion concerning an institute not *sui juris*.[58] It is also probable that a chapter is capable of introducing custom.[59] The province of an order may begin a custom according to Cicognani, in conformance with his definition that any community which can receive a true law, that is, a common precept, of its nature perpetual, may effect customary law.[60]

4. It is *more probable*, according to the majority of canonists, that a confraternity *cannot* produce customary law.[61] Practically all the definitions of canonists which explain the meaning of the community, spoken of in Canon 26, will deny that a sodality has the power to create a practice which leads to customary law.[62]

It is, therefore, concluded in general that a custom can be introduced by the Church universal, a province of an order, a diocese, a parish, a college of clerics.

C. *What Individuals of a Community?*

As long as the doctrine was tenable that a community with legislative power was subject of custom, it was likewise held that women,

Trummer, *Die Gewohnheit*, pp. 35-39; A Coronata, *Institutiones*, I, n. 39; Cappello, *Summa*, I, n. 112—deny that parishes are capable.

[56] Michiels, *loc. cit.*, and Kinane, *loc. cit.*, affirm it; Maroto, *Institutiones*, I, n. 180, denies it.

[57] Cicognani, *Jus can.*, II, 160.

[58] Michiels, *loc. cit.*, affirms this, but it is denied by Vermeersch-Creusen, *loc. cit.*, Maroto, *loc. cit.*, Cocchi, *loc. cit.*, and Cappello, *loc. cit.*

Vermeersch, who adopts the principle of perpetuity as the fundamental of his definition for a community capable of receiving law, illogically, it seems, admits a parish and not an institute. Since both are moral persons as indicated in Canon 531 and since all moral persons are *per se* perpetual according to Canon 102, § 1, it would seem that an institute is just as capable of receiving law as any parish.

[59] Cicognani, *loc. cit.*, Kinane, *loc. cit.*, Michiels, *loc. cit.*, admit a chapter. It is denied by Maroto, *loc. cit.*, Cocchi, *loc. cit.* A Coronata is doubtful concerning this, *loc. cit.*, while Trummer admits cathedral chapters, *loc. cit.*

[60] Cicognani, *loc. cit.*

[61] Maroto, *loc. cit.* Trummer, however, thinks that even a confraternity can do so, if it has pontifical approbation, *loc. cit.*

[62] Cappello, *loc. cit.*

minors, and the insane could not introduce a custom because they were without power to make law. With the changed understanding of the essence of custom, it soon became clear that both women and minors could introduce customs, since they are capable of human acts and fit subjects of law. Of course infants and the insane are still excluded (Canon 12). Commentators no longer admit that a community can consent to the acts of a minority and thereby introduce custom. Since it is taught no longer that the people's consent introduces custom, it is likewise affirmed that the legislator approves only acts performed by the majority.[63]

D. The Acts of the Community

(a) The Code does not intimate what kind of acts help to make a custom. It is clear, however, that not every kind of act plays a part. It would seem hardly necessary to say that the acts must be *free*. Yet a distinction is made by one writer between a custom beside the law and acts against the law. Concerning the former all are agreed that force and fear destroy the freedom of acts and prevent custom. Concerning the latter also it might be said that almost all agree.[64] Michiels admits that in a custom beside the law, acts which are not voluntary cannot become custom, since Canon 28 demands intention and consent. This is not demanded, however, by Canon 27, for a custom against the law, and, therefore, force and fear would not prevent such a custom. Michiels wrongly concludes, it seems, that absence of intention means that freedom need not be postulated.[65]

(b) The acts should also be *uniform* and *frequent*. It is clear that the various acts must be uniform to produce a legal norm. Only constant acts can show the mind of the majority concerning a definite observance. The same reasoning demands frequency of acts. The exact number of acts cannot be mathematically determined. Much will depend on circumstances.

[63] Augustine, *Commentary*, I, 107; Ojetti, *Comment.*, I, 174; Cocchi, *Comment.*, n. 135; Maroto, *Institutiones*, n. 252; Sägmüller, *Lehrbuch*, I, 166.

[64] Cappello, *Summa*, I, n. 113; Cicognani, *Jus can.*, II, 161; Ojetti, *Comment.*, I, 176; Maroto, *Institutiones*, I, 252.

[65] Michiels, *Normae Generales*, II, 49, note 2; *cf. infra* 112, where intention is considered.

(c) From the nature of the temporal duration, the so-called prescription, it may be gathered that the acts must be also *continuous*. This means that the acts must not be interrupted by contrary acts. Only serious and known interruptions would block the custom in the making. It has been suggested even that the interruption must be serious enough to cause a public disturbance and popular shock.[66]

(d) Finally the acts of the people must be *public*, either on the part of private persons or by judicial authority. The opinion that court sentences were necessary has long since been abandoned by the canonists. That law be introduced by way of custom, all the conditions can be fulfilled without court sentences.[67]

The more important qualities of the acts which form customary law will be treated in different sections of this study. Those characteristics which every custom must bear have just been studied, but the intention of the community, the knowledge of the people, the good or bad faith of the acts, must be considered under each specific kind of custom, because each represents distinct questions and calls for a corresponding discussion.

Article 5. The Reasonableness Demanded by Custom Against the Law

Canon 27, § 1. Iuri divino sive naturali sive positivo nulla consuetudo potest aliquatenus derogare; sed neque iuri ecclesiastico praeiudicium affert, nisi fuerit rationabilis et legitime per annos quadraginta continuos et completos praescripta; contra legem vero ecclesiasticam quae clausulam contineat futuras consuetudines prohibentem, sola praescribere potest rationabilis consuetudo centenaria aut immemorabilis.

§ 2. Consuetudo quae in iure expresse reprobatur, non est rationabilis.

[66] Some admit no interruption, Michiels, *Normae Generales*, II, 55; Trummer, *Die Gewohnheit*, p. 47. *Cf. supra* 55; Suarez, *de leg.*, c. 10, n. 4.

[67] *Cf. supra* 80, concerning the difference between the *stylus curiae* and custom.

A. Reasonableness—Custom's Relation to the Divine Law

Acts opposed to the natural law are said to be intrinsically evil. They are always and forever wrong. In the terminology of the moralist they are *prohibited because they are evil.* It follows then that there can never be a custom against the natural law.

The divine positive law has been expressed by a divine legislator. This law prohibits contrary acts. These arts are said to be extrinsically evil. They are *evil because they are prohibited.* It must be said that the divine lawmaker does not consent to a violation of laws, which He has instituted. Therefore no custom can abrogate the divine positive law.

B. Reasonableness—Custom's Relation to Ecclesiastical Law

Not only a custom against the divine natural or positive law, but also a custom against ecclesiastical law may be unreasonable. The legislator of Church law does not give any positive definition of what reasonableness may be. The only notion of reasonableness is found in the second number of Canon 27, which says that custom expressly reprobated in law is not reasonable. This negative definition recalls the words of Botonius and Hostiensis.[68] It might be asked why the legislator states when custom is not reasonable rather than affirming when a custom is reasonable. Should he not have given a positive definition and said that custom expressly approved is reasonable? Yet such a definition would not be all embracing, for even a custom not approved can be reasonable or can become reasonable. The lawgiver, therefore, says well that custom expressly reproved is not reasonable.

It must not be concluded from this that every custom not expressly reprobated is reasonable. Traditionally canonists have enumerated certain kinds of custom which must be considered unreasonable. Customs which upset Church discipline, which oppose the liberty of the Church, which occasion sin, in a word, which impede the Church from attaining her end are clearly unreasonable without express reprobation. These customs will often be infringements of even the divine positive law.

[68] *Cf. supra* 39.

An interesting response of the Sacred Congregation of the Council will help to explain the question of reprobation. There was a custom in a certain diocese whereby laymen acted as judges in matrimonial and other contentious cases. Laymen were also auditors in non-criminal cases. They were also allowed a consultative vote as assessors. It was claimed that this custom could boast the age of one hundred and seventy years. The question was asked whether such a custom could be sustained. The response of the Sacred Congregation of the Council noted that the Code affirms that laymen are incapable of spiritual jurisdiction (Canon 118). It also affirms the Church's competency in spiritual cases (Canon 1553) and restricts the exercise of the judicial function to priests (Canons 1573, 1574). Although the practice in question enjoyed a privileged age, it could not be considered as established, since it belonged in that class which the traditional expression says, "disrupts the nerve of ecclesiastical discipline," and opposes the liberty of the Church. If the approval of ecclesiastical superiors seems to have been given, it must be considered as forced from them by civil power.

Since the law before the Code allowed laymen to be assessors, the Sacred Congregation of the Council admitted that a centenary custom had been established and that the Ordinary, in accordance with Canon 5, might tolerate the practice, if it could not be removed prudently. But the response observes that even this practice should be abolished, if possible, since it is one of the customs which impedes the independence of the Church.[69]

Another case in point can be found in an answer of the Sacred Congregation of the Council concerning the *privilegium fori.* In Providence, Rhode Island, some Catholic laymen brought the bishop into civil court as a defendant. They had been clearly warned of the canonical penalty which they were in danger of incurring, yet without the permission of the Holy See they brought civil action against the bishop because of some of his official acts. When the matter was referred to the Sacred Congregation of the Council, the reply was made (*declarat*) that these laymen had incurred *ipso facto* the censure of Canon 2341. The declaration that the censure had been incurred

[69] S. C. C. *Resolutio, Wratislavien.*, 14 Dec., 1918—*AAS,* XI (1919), 128.

makes it clear that no custom in the United States existed contrary to the law. This answer implies that such a practice would not be recognized as reasonable, since it does not safeguard the freedom and dignity of the Church.[70]

It is clear that certain customs of their nature are unreasonable and it is equally evident that a custom expressly reprobated in law is not reasonable. But the question still remains to be answered how any custom against the law, even one not reprobated, can be reasonable when the law itself is supposed to be reasonable. A custom which is not intrinsically evil, is evil because it is prohibited. Its malice then depends, as it were, on the will of the legislator. The legislator then can take away the unreasonableness by admitting a custom under conditions which he places. And both the law and the contrary custom can be reasonable, because they are viewed from different ends. Custom against the law is reasonable for a particular situation, while the law itself remains an ordinance of reason for the general situation. A written law prohibiting poaching, for example, may be reasonable, but a custom against the law may be more reasonable for poor people living on the river's bank. When the legislator himself changes his law, he does not thereby admit that the law was unreasonable. There is no reason then why he cannot allow a reasonable custom to change a reasonable law.[71]

C. *Positive Utility*

It may be asked whether a custom must be more than negatively reasonable. Must it offer a positive contribution to the common good? The Code is silent concerning this question and some canonists are satisfied with negative reasonableness.[72]

Canonists who demand some positive utility in custom distinguish between the different kinds of custom. In a custom against the law, it would seem that general utility suffices. The mere fact of opposing the law would indicate that a community considers the law burden-

[70] S. C. C. (this decree bears no date)—*AAS*, XX (1928), 146.

[71] *Cf.* also *supra* 39, 52.

[72] Augustine, *Commentary*, I, 110; Cicognani, *Jus can.*, II, 163; Cocchi, *Comment.*, I, 136; A Coronata, *Institutiones*, I, n. 41.

some and that release from it will be for the common good.[73] A custom beside the law is not of necessity a contribution to the common good. The Code implies this by the use of the words *si pariter fuerit rationabilis* in the canon, which deals with custom beside the law.[74] A custom conformed to law will always promote the common good even as the law it interprets. It may be concluded in general that all customs must in some way defend, support, sustain or promote the common good.[75] The requirements for reasonableness in any custom may be regarded as summed up in the demand that a practice contribute the same utility to the common good, which a written law on the same matter, might offer.

D. The Judge of Reasonableness

The different kinds of custom enjoy various presumptions concerning their reasonableness. A universal custom is more readily considered reasonable than a particular custom. Custom conformed to law is always presumed reasonable. Custom against the law is not so easily presumed reasonable. Nor is custom beside the law to be presumed of necessity reasonable, since the legislator uses the words *pariter rationabilis* and since people are not prone to assume legal obligations.

In the final analysis, however, it always remains for the competent ecclesiastical superior to appraise the reasonableness of custom. A practical example might be cited to illustrate that the final judge of reasonableness is the legislator and that negative approbation may suffice for a custom. There is in a certain diocese a custom whereby pastors commit all High Mass intentions to curates. The curate celebrates the High Mass, for which he receives only the standard offering of a Low Mass. The balance is kept by the pastor, presumptively for the curate's board and keep. This practice would seem to be a violation of Canon 827, which condemns all species of barter and trade concerning stipends, or of Canon 840, which demands that stipends be transferred without dimunition.

[73] Michiels, *Normae Generales*, II, 89.

[74] *Cf. infra* 122, which treats of custom beside the law.

[75] Cappello, *Summa*, I, n. 114; Ojetti, *Comment.*, I, 180; Maroto, *Inst.*, I, n. 252; Vermeersch-Creusen, *Epitome*, I, n. 138.

Before the Code there was an ancient custom whereby some pastors demanded that the curate celebrate all Masses for their intention in order to compensate for board. This custom was tolerated at that time by the Holy See.[76] After the Code the Sacred Congregation replied to a somewhat similar situation:

> *Propositam consuetudinem remunerandi coadiutores vicarios* tolerari *posse*. Et ad mentem. Mens autem est quod "Administrator Apostolicus operam navet ut in praxi ponatur statutum diocesanum vi cuius parochi cooperatoribus suis mercedem solvant 25 ponderum, adiecto quotidie missae stipendio integro iuxta taxam, ita ut honorarium menstruum summae 50 ponderum coaequetur.[77]

This decision of the Sacred Congregation then tolerates an arrangement of stipends distinct from board and salary, rather than the former practice which granted a lump sum of fifty pesos to assistants. It cannot be concluded that the legislator has condemned the custom mentioned as seemingly contrary to Canons 827 or 840. When a chance was given the legislator to recognize positively the reasonableness of such a custom, the reply was "it may be tolerated." Since the final judge of a custom is the superior this negative approbation is enough to leave the custom reasonable. But this approbation does not encourage the formation of similar customs.[78]

Another example to show that the final judge of a custom is the legislator may be presented by the case following. In a reply given concerning Canon 788 the Code Commission had said that in the Latin Church the sacrament of confirmation cannot be conferred before the age of about seven years, except in the cases mentioned in that canon.[79]

In Spain, however, and in South America there had long been a custom of administering the sacrament of confirmation to children immediately after baptism. The Sacred Congregation of the Sacraments was asked, therefore, if this custom could be sustained. The reply was given in the affirmative, but at the same time it was said

[76] S. C. C. *decr.*, 25 Feb., 1905—*ASS*, XXXVIII (1905), 16.

[77] S. C. C. *Montisvidei et Aliarum*, 10 Jan., 1920—*AAS*, XII (1920), 70-73.

[78] *Cf.* Keller, *Mass Stipends*, 1926; p. 85.

[79] *Cod. Com.*, 16 June, 1931—*AAS*, XXIII (1931), 353.

that confirmation should be postponed until about the age of seven, unless grave and just causes prevented this course of action. At the same time the faithful should be taught the law of Canon 788 and by catechetical instruction informed concerning the nature and effects of the sacrament of confirmation.[80]

E. *Reprobating Clauses*

There are three kinds of clauses which the legislator sometimes appends to his laws, when speaking of custom. One is called a prohibitory clause. This phrase puts more restrictions, greater barriers against a practice, which it must surmount if it is to become customary law. It does not, however, call the practice unreasonable.[81] A second kind of clause is known as a revocatory clause. This connotes merely that the lawgiver thinks that a particular custom should be abolished for the common good. The phrase abrogates the custom involved, but it does not declare that the practice is unreasonable.[82]

A third type of clause is called the reprobating clause. This phraseology affirms that a certain usage is unreasonable. When a legislator reprobates a custom, he may say that it is always and forever wrong, unreasonable by its very nature. Such an affirmation is said to be a *declarative* reprobation, and it affects both past customs, which seemed to have been established, and any future practice contrary to the law.

There may be other reasons which in the mind of the legislator prompt the reprobation of a certain practice. When he defines, therefore that, as far as the positive law is concerned, a particular custom is not reasonable, his condemnation is called *dispositive*. This kind of condemnation, unlike the declarative reprobation, does not of necessity take away established customs, while it declares such practice as unreasonable for the future. This is explained by an example.

The Sacred Congregation of the Sacraments was asked a number of questions by the Archbishop of Utrecht concerning the sponsors in baptism. A practice existed whereby the person chosen to be

[80] S. C. Sacr. *Reply*, 30 June, 1932—*AAS*, XXIV (1932), 271.

[81] This kind of clause is treated under prescription. *Cf. infra* 119.

[82] This clause will be treated under cessation. *Cf. infra* 136.

sponsor for an infant, whose baptism he could not attend, was represented by proxy. The absent person, according to the practice, did not give any express mandate to a representative. Rather the minister of baptism or the parents were accustomed to designate some other person to be proxy. According to Canon 765, 5° there must be a physical contact between the one baptized and the sponsor, or proxy, during the act of baptism. Because of this custom then the Archbishop asked the Congregation what was necessary to establish a proxy according to law and whether in the custom under consideratin the impediment of spiritual relationship had been contracted (Canon 1079). The reply of the Sacred Congregation was that if the sponsor, knowing of the custom, intends to conform to it, he does contract the spiritual relationship, if he is otherwise canonically qualified according to Canon 765. The Congregation, therefore, sustained the custom for the past and then proceded to give various reasons why it *is to be reprobated* for the future. It was stated that such a custom prevented the sponsor from having full consciousness of his obligation, that it prevented the pastor from investigating concerning the validity and liceity of the sponsorship and that it left a grave matter in uncertainty and doubt.[83]

The instruction of the Sacred Congregation, which the above question provoked said, " . . . the Eminent Fathers of this Sacred Congregation of the Sacraments, while they replied to the question submitted by saying that a spiritual *relationship is contracted* when the thing is done in the manner described in the question, yet they at the same time sharply reproved the aforesaid custom."

This then is a clear example of a dispositive reprobation which sustains a past custom and reprobates the practice for the future.[84]

When a legislator reprobates a custom in a dispositive manner he affirms it unreasonable from the point of view of his law and the common good. Since this kind of reprobation is not declarative and does not mean that the very nature of the custom is unreason-

[83] S. C. de Sacr. *Ultraiecten, De patrinis baptismatis*, 24 July, 1925—*AAS*, XVIII (1926), 43-47.

[84] S. C. de Sacr. *Instructio*, 25 Nov., 1925—*AAS*, XVIII (1926), 44-47; *cf.* also *Cod. Com.*, 12 Nov., 1922—*AAS*, XIV (1922), 662, which speaks of the cumulative right to a baptismal font.

able, the question arises whether the practice can ever become reasonable. Some are of the opinion that such a usage can never become reasonable.[85]

It is also affirmed, however, that there is a possibility that a practice once condemned by a dispositive reprobation can become reasonable. It must be remembered, nevertheless, that this can never be effected until the practice has received the consent of the legislator, which in fact amounts to a revocation of the reprobation. If a special consent is given, it seems evident that the lawmaker no longer considers the usage unreasonable. But those who hold this opinion add that even with only the legal approval of the legislator the practice can become reasonable. They argue that the condemnation is to be considered as given because of certain present circumstances. And, therefore, they say, when the background of the circumstances which cause the reprobation of the custom changes, then it becomes possible for the custom to be invested with such qualities which no longer will brand it as unreasonable.[86]

It may be admitted that the question under consideration is more theoretical than practical. It seems that if a custom once condemned has undergone a change of circumstances so that the cause of its reprobation has ceased, the usage can hardly be called the same custom. If, on the other hand, there is a change in the mind of the legislator, so that he later considers reasonable what he once condemned, then even in his judgment there has been a change and the custom is only factually the same, not juridically.

It must be noted, however, that it is not so likely that a reprobation be rendered useless. Since laws are the product of much time and thought and since reprobating clauses are not placed against practices haphazardly, it can safely be said that a custom once reprobated cannot become reasonable and must be considered as corruption of law. Such a practice cannot revive because its very entrance upon a period of possible temporal prescription remains perpetually excluded.

[85] Cicognani, *Jus can.*, II, 32 and 166; Ojetti, *Comment.*, I, 63 and 185.

[86] Cappello, *Summa*, I, n. 114; Trummer, *Die Gewohnheit*, p. 77.

The usual formula employed to express reprobation is *reprobata consuetudine contraria.* Sometimes the addition of such modifiers as *quavis, quacumque,* or *qualibet* in relation to custom supplement the reprobative clause with an external manifestation of incisiveness.

The force of an abrogatory clause is well exemplified in a reply given concerning a certain Spanish custom. For more than one hundred years there was a custom in Spain whereby all the canons who were present in choir for one of the canonical hours daily, were counted as present for the purpose of receiving the prebends of the endowments. Only those who were actually present, however, partook of the daily distributions for each canonical hour. The Sacred Congregation replied that the Spanish custom, even though centenary and immemorial, could not be sustained and tolerated. The words *reprobata contraria consuetudine* of Canon 418 reprobates the custom by which prebendaries received prebends when canonically absent from choir.[87]

Scattered throughout the Code are many laws which contain reprobative clauses. Such clauses are found in the following canons: In the laws which deal with the bishop's canonical visitation (Canons 343, § 2, 346), the question of option in chapters (Canon 396, § 2), the conferring of certain benefices (Canon 403), the use of choral attire or special insignia by capitularies when outside their diocese (Canon 409, § 2), the duration of the annual vacation granted to canons and beneficiaries of cathedral and collegiate chapters (Canon 418, § 1), the election of only one vicar capitular or administrator to be the sole and only incumbent as diocesan Ordinary (Canon 433, § 1), the naming of pastors (Canon 455, § 1), the exclusive authority of a single pastor in a single parish (Canon 460, § 2), the need of a baptismal font in every parish (Canon 744, § 1), the compliance with the rubrics of the Mass (Canon 818), the observance of the interstices of ordination (Canon 978, § 3), the use of proper times or season for the conferring of sacred orders (Canon 1006, § 5), the introduction of new matrimonial impediments as well as the abolishing of existing ones (Canon 1041), the collection of gainful fees in the

[87] S. C. C. *Resolutio, Toletana et aliarum,* 10 July, 1920—*AAS,* XXII (1920), 357-365.

granting of matrimonial dispensations (Canon 1056), the free admission of worshipers to church (Canon 1181), the discharge of assessments demanded for the seminary (Canon 1356, § 1), the requirement of the public profession of faith (Canon 1408), the submission of a report to the local Ordinary by exempt pious institutes (Canon 1492, § 1), the annual forwarding of a report of the administration of churches, confraternities, religious and charitable institues (Canon 1525, § 1), the required number of judges designated for particular issues (Canon 1576, § 1).

Article 6. The Question of Intention in Custom Against the Law

Although it has been shown that the legal force of custom rests with the consent of the ruler, it must not be forgotten that the people originate custom in so far as they present the material of the custom to the ruler for his consent. It may be asked, then, if the people must have the intention to produce a legal obligation while they are performing the acts. The Code has nothing to say concerning intention when it deals with a custom against the law. It is clear that the words *"cum animo se obligandi"* are found in Canon 28, which deals with custom beside the law, while Canon 27, which concerns customs against the law, omits these words.

1. In spite of this omission the more common opinion demands intention even for custom against the law. The difference in the texts of Canons 27 and 28, it is affirmed, can be admitted, but silence in the Code is no argument. The Code, it is said, in no way attempts to furnish an exhaustive treatment of the canonical concept of custom. Many questions concerning customary law are not even mentioned in this title. The five canons leave much to the teaching of the canonists. All this is clearly provided for in Canon 6, which tells us to interpret the law in its historical setting, when it is repeated substantially. It seems then that Canon 27 should follow the decretal *Quum Tanto* of Gregory IX, and the tradition of the doctors. The common opinion before the Code was that intent is required even for a custom against the law. Even in doubt about the agreement of the later with the earlier law the legislator favors the past (Canon 6, 4°). It seems certain that the lawmaker would

not wish to reverse the opinion of the ages without clearly saying so. It may be admitted that a ruler could consent to a custom without the people intending to establish one. But there is no proof that the lawgiver is always willing that this law be abrogated, or that he intends to consent to a custom which the people perform in ignorance, in error, or without intention. Historically it has been demonstrated that the Church has not been more eager to release her subjects from law, than she has been desirous of accepting new customs. The opinion, therefore, which seems to be the more common, demands that the community have the intention to abolish the law, when it acts against the statutes.[88]

2. But the opposite opinion, though less commonly held, seems to be more solidly founded. This doctrine maintains that the legislator purposely omitted the words *"cum animo"* from his canon, because he does not demand intention when the community acts against the law. The very nature of custom, it continues, does not demand the intention in the people. Since it has been established that a custom receives its legal force, not from the people, but from the legislator, there is no need to demand that the people have the intention of inducing law. The lawgiver realizes this and purposely omits the note of intention when he deals with custom against his law. He does not wish to hold people to an imprudent law, if they are manifestly unwilling to obey it. Moreover, it should not be forgotten that the title of the Code, which deals with custom, is giving *conditions* necessary to establish a custom. Therefore, the silence of the Code in respect of certain prospective conditions for the establishment of customary law seems to be especially significant. As will soon be seen, there is a great difference between the acquisition and assumption of a new obligation on the one hand (*per consuetudinem praeter legem*) and the nullification or liberation from an obligation inherent in law on the other hand (*per consuetudinem contra legem*). It will become immediately apparent that the former opinion is decidedly at a disadvantage when trying to reconcile the elements of error and intention in the formation of custom. It is equally manifest

[88] Van Hove, *De consuet.*, nn. 124-127; Cappello, *Summa*, n. 113; Cicognani, *Jus can.*, II, 161; Maroto, *Inst.*, I, 252; Wehrle, *De la coutume*, p. 412; Cocchi, *Comment.*, I, 135.

that the lenient opinion can firmly rely on the wording of Canon 27 to plead the logic of its position and that it receives reënforcement from Canon 28, which expressly adds *scienter . . . cum animo se obligandi* for the development of custom outside the law.

Article 7. The Question of Error in Custom Against the Law

Closely connected with the question of intention is the notion of error in custom against the law. It will be important, therefore, to remember what has been just investigated in the preceding article, namely, that one opinion demands intention in custom against the law and another, which the writer sponsors, does not require it.

It is noted that Canon 28 contains the word *scienter,* while Canon 27 omits it. The question is then whether the Code still demands knowledge on the part of the community, or a consciousness that it is abolishing a law and creating a new legal obligation. Because of the silence of Canon 27, there are various opinions concerning error in a custom, which is meant to abrogate law.

1. Some demand of custom against the law the same knowledge required by Canon 28 for custom beside the law. They would add *scienter* to Canon 27 also. This opinion excludes the possibility of any error, because it likewise holds the doctrine that there must be an intention to abolish law. How, it is asked, can there be an intention to free oneself from the law, if there is error concerning the very existence of the law? This opinion argues for the need of knowledge both to abolish law and to establish law. Our particular concern here is rather a custom against the law than a custom beside the law, which will be treated more specifically later. But it will be useful to examine here the double hypothesis, which this opinion offers. Either a law really exists or it does not exist. If the law does not exist and the people think that it does, if, for example, people in the United States think that St. Patrick's Day is a holyday of obligation and consequently go to Mass, they cannot, says this opinion, produce a custom thereby. In their error they could not have the intention to establish by custom a law, which they really think already exists. If, on the other hand, the law really does exist, while the people think that it does not, if, for example, the people mistakenly think

that Wednesdays of Lent are not days of abstinence in the United States, and, therefore, do not observe them, they cannot abolish the law because again intention is lacking. Since they think that a law is non-existent, they cannot will to abrogate that law. This opinion, therefore, which demands in a community the intent to abolish law, likewise in consequence thinks it necessary to exclude the possibility of all error.[89]

2. A second opinion which likewise demands the presence of intention in a community, nevertheless admits the possibility of some error. To sustain its position this doctrine distinguishes between two kinds of error, that which is called antecedent and that which is known as concomitant. Before proceeding with this opinion it will be necessary to explain these two kinds of error somewhat more thoroughly.

Error might be defined as the false apprehension of truth. The error is called antecedent, when it is the sole cause of action; it is related to the action as cause to the effect. When the relation of cause and effect is not so involved the error is called concomitant. With this distinction in mind the opinion continues.

If the one and only reason (antecedent error) for which a community acts against the law is based on error, there is no possibility of having an intention and of introducing custom. In such a case an unknown law could not be considered odious and undesired by the people. Since antecedent error involves a connection so intimate as cause and effect, such error on the part of a community could in no way effect the necessary will to free oneself from the law.

But when a people pertinaciously do not keep a law for some time, there would seem to be a combination of causes for their action. They might indeed be in error, but it would not be the sole cause of their action against the law. The error would be only concomitant without influencing the popular action as cause influences effect.

Indeed, this opinion continues, if all error is excluded from the evolving custom for the entire time prescribed, few customs would arise, for in the course of time error easily arises concerning the very existence of a law long not obeyed.

89 Maroto, *Inst.*, I, n. 252; Sägmüller, *Lehrbuch des Katholischen Kirchenrechts*, I, p. 166.

This opinion, therefore, demands intention and yet admits the presence of concomitant error. How can these two positions be reconciled? In order to reconcile the presence of error with intention in a community, this opinion must invoke what is known as the interpretative intention. This kind of intention is a presumption of what the people would do if they were not in error concerning the law. Some laws may be useless, if not evil, in given circumstances. The fact that a community over a long time acts contrary to the law would indicate this. It does not matter that the people do not know of the law's existence. The prolonged contrary action itself argues that even if the law were known the people would disobey it. This intention which is found in the minds of the people along with the error which is not the sole cause of their action, is called the interpretative intent. It is admitted by the proponents of this doctrine that this kind of intention is no real intention, but, it is said, the intention becomes efficacious with the permission or approbation of the legislator, who, after all, is the one to determine the conditions of customary law. It is further suggested that an ecclesiastical legislator acts wisely in consenting to the interpretative intention of popular action, for when a community for a long period of time does not keep a law, it is rather easy to presume this interpretative intent.[90]

3. It is to be recalled once more that this question of error is closely connected with the doctrine concerning intention in the community. The first two opinions, which have just been considered, both demanded intention. Because they required this intention, the first excluded the possibility of any error; the second admitted concomitant error and attempted to reconcile it with intention by the doctrine of the interpretative intent. This third opinion, however, is free from the difficulties, which the first two encounter. This doctrine admits the presence of all kinds of error in custom against the law. But since the protagonists of this teaching do not demand intention in a community, they have no difficulty in trying to reconcile error with intention. This opinion seems to have more merit than the others for several reasons.

[90] Cappello, *Summa*, n. 113; Ojetti, *Comment.*, I, p. 183; Van Hove, *De consuet.*, nn. 142, 143.

It is certainly more than a coincidence that both the word *animo* and the word *scienter* are omitted in the law which speaks of custom contrary to law, while they are inserted in the canon which treats of custom beside the law. Adherents to the other opinions will note that the more common tradition demanded knowledge on the part of a community and that mere silence on the part of the canons would not abolish the traditional doctrine. However, when the lawmaker is clearly giving the conditions which he demands in customary law, it seems that his silence discloses his will. When the legislator omits two pregnant words, such as *animo* and *scienter,* in one canon and inserts them in the other, his silence must be considered deliberate. The lawmaker acts negatively indeed, but none the less efficaciously.

The second merit of this opinion is that it has no need to have recourse to a figment of the mind, the so-called interpretative intention, in order to reconcile error and intent. The doctrine of the interpretative intention must find its efficacy in the approbation of the legislator given to acts performed against his will. In reality then the interpretative intention becomes no intention at all. It seems much better to read the mind of the legislator in his own law and to demand neither knowledge nor intention.

If it may be permitted to summarize a very complex question for the reader, the picture in brief is this. There are three opinions concerning error in custom against the law. The first will admit no error, since it demands in a community an intention to abolish law. The second will admit concomitant error, and it safeguards intention, which it demands, by invoking the doctrine of interpretative intent. The third opinion admits all error and does not require an intention. This last doctrine the writer sponsors for the reasons just explained.[91]

Article 8. The Question of Good or Bad Faith in Custom Against the Law

The use of the words *legitime praescripta* does not refer to prescription, but only to the temporal duration of the formative cus-

[91] Michiels, *Normae Generales,* II, 65-69.

tom. It is false then to imagine that the legislator demands of custom all those qualities which are needed in prescription. The Code provides for prescription in Canon 1512, when it says:

> Nulla valet praescriptio, nisi bona fide nitatur, non solum initio possessionis, sed toto possessionis tempore ad praescriptionem requisito.

Real prescription requires good faith for the very good reason that if prescription were legitimate in bad faith, the innocent would be in danger of suffering more frequent temporal loss. In custom, however, this reason is not present, since custom purposes to establish a real law, which has for its object the common good. The canons of the Code then which demand good faith in real prescription do not refer to Canons 25-30, which deal with custom. The question may still be asked, therefore, whether the community that begins by practice to establish a custom must be in good faith.

1. At first thought it might seem that a community must be in good faith to begin a custom. It would seem that an act against the law, when placed in bad faith, is unreasonable. It will be important, however, to remember that in the study of reasonableness it was also pointed out that there is a difference between an act intrinsically wrong and one extrinsically wrong.[92] It was shown that there can be no custom against the divine law. But the reasonableness of any custom against a positive human law depends upon the human legislator. For just as the lawgiver himself could change his law and make it be in harmony with the acts of a community, which were formerly contrary to the law, so also custom can do likewise.

Acts placed in bad faith, therefore, are not of necessity unreasonable, although they may be sinful. When the legislator then admits bad faith, does he not condone sin? When an act is placed by a community in bad faith there are two elements to be considered. First of all there is the evil of disobeying the enactment of the legislator. But secondly there is the question of the common good. When a law has been consistently disobeyed for a long period of time by a majority there is at least an indication that such a law is too burdensome on human nature. The common good then would seem to

[92] *Cf. supra* 99.

demand that such an impractical enactment should be removed from the shoulders of the people. And so when a legislator condones bad faith, when he tolerates sins against his canons, he considers the double effect of such actions. The one effect which may be sinful, if there be bad faith in a community, he does not favor for its own sake. But he sees rather the greater good, the popular utility which is manifested in the acts of a community. It is this that he favors, since he knows that paradoxically, by sin the dangers of sin may be lessened, for an intolerable law is an occasion of sin. It may be concluded then that bad faith can be present in the acts of a community. Does this mean that bad faith is always present?

2. In establishing custom a community need not be in good faith. Is it, therefore, necessary that the acts be placed always in bad faith? This question is connected with the doctrine, already explained, concerning the intention needed by a community. Canonists will again divide in the solution of this matter, according to whether they demand intention or think that no intention is needed.

(a) It would seem, at first, that those who demand intention must hereby require also bad faith in a community. In order that a community intend to abolish a law, it seems necessary that the persons violate that law in bad faith. These canonists, however, maintain that good faith can exist along with an interpretative intention. "Bad faith is not always the first cause of acting against the law. There may be a thorough conviction that a law is no longer useful or adapted to circumstances, and hence had better be disregarded. Besides, it must be maintained that the people directly and reflexly have the will only of freeing themselves from a burden or a restriction opposed to liberty, which reflexive will cannot be said to be evil in itself. Therefore, bad faith must not necessarily be supposed; and even if it were present in the beginning it may disappear afterwards." [93] The question of interpretative intention has been investigated in the preceding article.[94]

There it was shown that an interpretative intention is one which is presumed in the mind of a people. Its efficacy comes from the will of the legislator. If priests, for example, in a certain country

[93] Augustine, *Commentary*, I, 108.

[94] *Cf. supra* 111, 112.

should fail to wear a biretta at Mass, because they think there is no law obliging the practice, they would evidently be in good faith. But, if they are in good faith, how can they intend to abolish the law? The doctrine of the interpretative intention says that probably the community would act in the same way, even if it knew of the law's existence. And so, this opinion teaches that good faith and interpretative intention can be present together.[95]

(b) On the other hand, those canonists who do not require any intention in the community are again free from the difficulty of reconciling good faith with intention. Neither good nor bad faith embarrasses this opinion. If the community be in bad faith and clearly intends to abolish the law, no reconciliation of the concepts is needed. If the community be in good faith, there is no need to invoke the interpretative intention, which is really no intention. This opinion merely says that the law demands no intention.[96]

Article 9. The Prescription of Custom Against the Law

1. The words *legitime praescripta,* which are found in Canon 27, do not signify real prescription, although they have been borrowed from the concept of true prescription. Some think that the Code retains these words in the sense that the custom must measure up to the conditions prescribed by law; others believe that it means a long custom. More properly it signifies, what it has meant traditionally, that the custom must run through a duration of time fixed by law. The words do not imply true prescription. The only points which custom and prescription have in common is that each demands usage over a period of time and that custom, like prescription, may on occasions produce subjective rights by conferring a privilege (Canon 63, § 1). The many essential differences, studied throughout the historical part of this work, make it clear that custom is not real prescription. The legislator of the Code speaks of prescription in Canon 1508 which canonizes civil law; in Canon 1509 which gives

[95] Van Hove, *De consuet.*, n. 156; Ojetti, *Comment.*, I, 183; Toso, *Comment. min.*, I, 86; Cappello, *Summa*, I, n. 113.

[96] Michiels, *Normae Generales*, II, 68; Trummer, *Die Gewohnheit*, p. 135.

the subject and the object of prescription; in Canon 1511, which demands one hundred years for prescription against the Holy See, and thirty years against other moral persons in the Church. It is certain that these canons have no reference to the second title of the first book of the Code.

2. A practice then must run for a prescribed time in order to become law. Before the Code there was much debate concerning the length of time needed by a practice in order that it become customary law. The Code has settled all doubt by stating clearly that custom against the law must have a duration of forty years to become established. The source of this law is the decretal *Quum Tanto* of Gregory IX,[97] which applies to universal laws only. Because of this it has been objected that Canon 27 does not refer to particular laws, but only to general laws. Commentators, however, both before and after the Code have long since applied the principles of both the decretal *Quum Tanto* and Canon 27 to custom which is contrary to particular law. Approved authors then agree that the legislation of the Code regulates customs against all laws, particular and universal.

3. In accordance with the traditional doctrine, a custom may receive the special consent of the legislator. This consent, as has been explained,[98] may be either expressed or tacit. When a custom receives such consent, does it nevertheless need forty years' duration in order that it obtain force of law?

An argument might be attempted from the silence of the Code concerning any other norm than forty years for abolishing a law by custom. Silence might indicate that the legislator does not intend to give his consent to any custom less than forty years of age. However, when the Code established the norm of forty years for legal consent, the legislator did not thereby relinquish his power to give a special consent before that time. It seems clear that Canon 25 by using the word *competentis* [99] at least indicates the possibility of a consent, in which there is no need of the forty years spoken of by the subsequent Canons 27 and 28, which deal with legal consent.

[97] *Cf. supra* 23.

[98] *Cf. supra* 83.

[99] Consuetudo in Ecclesia vim legis a consensu *competentis* Superioris ecclesiastici unice obtinet (Canon 25).

Although the possibility of a special consent is upheld, it must not be imagined that custom requires no time at all to be established. The part of the people in customary law must not be overlooked. It is merely affirmed that when special consent is given, a custom does not need the forty years which legal consent demands, that the practice needs no *determined* time. But there must be *some duration* of time, some multiplication of acts on the part of a community. If there were not this succession of popular acts, the special consent of a lawmaker would not confirm customary law which is a product of the people, but it would rather enact a law of his own. It is, therefore, concluded that a custom against the law may receive the special approval of the legislator and that with this approval the acts of a community may create a custom in less time than forty years.

4. It may be asked now at what point the required time begins to run its course. Must all the elements enumerated in this study be present from the beginning? Practically, it seems that the normal custom begins without any thought about establishing customary law. In time these acts come to be used by the majority and are established as common practice, while the common intention grows out of the usage. Although the early acts are not simultaneous with intention, they really form part of the common practice and should be computed.[100]

5. At times custom may oppose the rights of an individual, or the very acts may be the product of an individual and not of a community. Such situations seem to cause a confusion between real prescription and custom. Must these acts then follow the rules of prescription or must they realize the qualities of legitimate custom? The answer is disjunctive. Either the acts have attained all the neccessary conditions for custom or they have not. If no real custom has been established thus far, the only other question at hand is whether there is place for true prescription. This must be judged according to Canons 1508-1512. But what is to be said, if the legitimate custom has been established already and this custom attacks the rights of an individual? The answer can be found in a decision of the Sacred Congregation of the Council. In the Dio-

[100] Van Hove, *De consuet.*, n. 193.

cese of Gallipolis the cathedral Chapter had the custom of retaining the pastor's portion of funeral fees. Canon 1236, § 1, provides: "Without prejudice to particular laws which may provide otherwise, when the deceased is not buried from his own parish church, the pastor's portion is due to the deceased's own pastor, except in the case where the body cannot conveniently be brought to the deceased's own parish church." In the case in point it is admitted that the custom is a violation of this law, but an attempt is made to justify it on the plea that it is an immemorial custom. The Sacred Congregation of the Council, however, did not overlook the pastor's right in this matter. It was decided that custom alone could not violate his right, but that all the conditions of real prescription were necessary. Since these conditions were absent, the custom, even immemorial, could not extinguish the pastor's right and he is entitled to the canonical portion of the funeral fees.[101]

6. Customs against prohibiting clauses.

The concluding words of Canon 27 say that a custom must be centenary or immemorial to abolish a law which contains a prohibiting clause. The Code itself contains no such clause in any of its canons. This is the first legal ruling concerning this kind of clause. The prohibitory clause is not the same as the reprobatory clause studied under the chapter on reasonableness, nor does the latter in any way contain the former. Indeed this very law shows that the prohibitory clause does not touch reasonableness since it says plainly that the custom against it must be reasonable. The phrase of Canon 5 *"neve sinantur in posterum reviviscere"* does not eventuate into a prohibiting clause, as some would teach.[102] Those canons which state what is known as a *lex irritans* do not thereby contain what is equivalent to a prohibiting clause. Normally this type of clause affects only the future; it may include also the present growing customs if it is clearly so worded.[103] This law then offers an exception to the forty years norm demanded for other customs

101 *Cf.* S. C. C. *Resolutio, Gallipolitana,* 25 May and 15 Nov., 1930—*AAS,* XXV (1933), 155-159.

102 *Cf. supra* 74; Michiels, *Normae Generales,* I, 77; Trummer, *Die Gewohnheit,* p. 156.

103 Cicognani, *Jus can.,* II, 165; Trummer, *Die Gewohnheit,* p. 155.

and it states that time immemorial or a centenary custom is needed to abrogate a law with a prohibiting clause. Whether the word "*aut*" indicates a distinction between a centenary custom and an immemorable custom has been studied elsewhere in connection with the word "*et*" of Canon 5.[104] This legislation, of course, applies only to legal consent. If the lawmaker gives his special consent to the practice, the prohibition is taken away and the custom need not be centenary or immemorial.

Article 10. Are There Any Laws Which Custom Cannot Abrogate?

A. Laws of the Code, Which Originated in the Council of Trent

The Code has properly retained much legislation from the past within its canons. Many things which are established in the legislation of the Code were born in the Council of Trent. Of the many laws which came from the greatest council of all times, some have been maintained in the codification with little or no change. According to Canon 6 these laws should be appraised in the light of the old law. It is claimed, therefore, that the historical controversy concerning customs opposed to the Council of Trent is still on the floor of debate.[105]

It is more correctly affirmed, however, that the question is historical and nothing more. Only if the Code repeats certain reprobating clauses, once used by Trent, could it be said to retain the old law and forbid custom from abrogating it. Certainly custom which the Council of Trent had called intrinsically evil cannot revive under the Code or under heaven. Even if the Pope by a general indictment (which is to be denied) had reprobated all customs against the Council of Trent, that law no longer exists in the Code. Nor does a *stylus* exist which reprobates such custom. If it did exist, it would refer rather to the Tridentine legislation, than to the Code.[106]

[104] *Cf. supra* 74.

[105] Michiels, *Normae Generales*, II, 105. For a consideration of the study of this question in the past, *cf. supra* 54.

[106] Van Hove, *De consuet.*, n. 229.

B. Liturgical Laws

The liturgy has long been held sacred in the Church. Historically, therefore, even in the days of the *Corpus Juris Canonici,* the question was asked whether a custom could ever oppose liturgical law.[107] After the advent of the Code, it is still debated whether the principles of customary law are to be applied to the liturgy. Only a few canons in the Code offer any suggestion. Canon 2 says that the rules about rites and ceremonies retain all their force unless they are expressly corrected in the Code. Codification of liturgical laws was not part of the legislator's plan. Canon 6 affirms that all liturgical laws remain in force and need not be renewed individually. Canon 31 maintains liturgical rules in computing time. Canon 253 confines the competency of the Sacred Congregation of Rites to rites and ceremonies. It is not competent concerning legal principles. Canon 818 reprobates customs contrary to the rubrics of the Mass. None of these canons then indicates that liturgy is any exception to the principles of Book I, Title II. Even this canon which treats of the Holy Sacrifice does not differ from any canon, which might contain a reprobating clause. There are then no special rules for liturgical laws, no exceptions to the *normae generales.*

Since liturgical law follows the regular principles of customary law, custom against it would be prohibited, as against any other law, if it could be demonstrated that the consent of the legislator is denied or that the custom is unreasonable. It cannot be proved that this has happened to all liturgical customs.

Although a particular condemnation can easily be found for various customs, the practice of the Sacred Congregation of Rites indicates that there is no law which prohibts, reprobates or abrogates all customs against the liturgy. Indeed even a cursory reading under the word *consuetudo* of the index of the *Decreta Authentica* demonstrates the contrary. The Sacred Congregation admits customs against the liturgy, receiving them with various degrees of judicial phraseology. It accepts some customs with the comment *pro gratia, facto verbo cum Sanctissimo, indulsit, non esse inquiet-*

[107] *Cf.* c. 3, *de aetate et qualitate et ordine promovendorum,* I, 6, in Clem.; Suarez, *de leg.,* L. VII, c. 19, n. 25; Schmalzgrueber, lib. I, tit. IV, n. 21.

andos. Others it calls *laudabiles*. Nay more sometimes the Congregation uses the words *indulsit et servari mandavit*.[108] The action of the Congregation in condemning or tolerating customs is nothing more than the application of the regular principles of customary law. They show no special rules for the liturgy. It may be said, perhaps, that the reprobation of such customs are more frequent. If this be true, it is partly because liturgy is closely associated with doctrine and morals and the legislator is fearful of anything that might weaken dogmatic unity. It may be concluded nevertheless, that a custom can abolish laws prescribed by liturgy.[109]

Article 11. Custom Beside the Law

Canon 28. Consuetudo praeter legem quae scienter a communitate cum animo se obligandi servata sit legem inducit, si pariter fuerit rationabilis et legitime per annos quadraginta continuos et completos praescripta.

1. *Reasonableness in Custom Beside the Law*

This canon offers the first general law concerning a custom beside the law. Although canonists had studied this kind of custom, the legislation of the Decretals had made no law concerning it. It will be noticed that this canon has the word "*pariter*" which is not found in Canon 27. The legislator evidently intends to indicate that a custom arising outside the law should have some positive reasonableness, a positive contribution towards the common good.[110] This means that not every practice existing beside the law is to be accepted as a reasonable legal obligation. This recalls the idea, already expressed by St. Augustine,[111] that useless customs are not

[108] *Cf. Decreta authentica* S. C. R. *ad verbum "consuetudo,"* nn. 154, 184, 218, 299, 2935, 3046, 3127, 3145, 3248, 3413, 3991, 4270.

[109] A. De Meester, *Iuris canonici et iuris canonico-civilis compendium*, I, Brugis, 1921; C. Callewaert, *Liturgicae institutiones*, I, *De sacra liturgia universim;* Victorius ab Appeltern, "De consuetudine contra leges liturgicas juxta novum codicem juris canonici," *Ephemerides liturgicae*, XXXI (1917), 430 ff., 558 ff.; Vermeersch-Creusen, *Epitome*, I, n. 143.

[110] Trummer, *Die Gewohnheit*, pp. 83-85.

[111] *Cf. supra* 6.

to be multiplied in the Church. It has been shown historically that many laws originated in custom. Although useless customs are not to be multiplied, the practice of the people outside the statute law is the best guide for new legislation. The laws of fast and abstinence, for example, the diriment impediments of matrimony, the law of celibacy, the divine office and many other legal obligations began in custom.

It seems that even a custom coming into existence beside the law may be reprobated as unreasonable. Canon 1041, which forbids the formation of new matrimonial impediments, offers such an example.

2. *The Question of Intention in Custom Beside the Law*

It has been seen that the silence of Canon 27 has caused a difference of opinion concerning the community's intention in a custom against the law. Canon 28, however, which deals with a custom beside the law says clearly that a practice must be introduced *cum animo se obligandi.* Because of the clarity of the law canonists are agreed concerning the need of intention for a community to produce a new obligation.

In as much as the custom is outside the law, the legislator does not wish to impose a new obligation by way of custom, unless the community itself really asks for it. If the legislator had wished to do so, he would have made statute law. It has been said that all canonists demand intention for this kind of custom, but they are divided on the reason why intent is needed.

Michiels consistently maintains that intention is no more demanded here *from the very nature of custom* than in a custom against the law. But it is the kindness of the lawmaker, who does not wish to burden an unwilling people, that demands intention in custom beside the law.[112]

On the other side it is maintained that the nature of custom itself requires an intention, even if the legislator did not demand it. And the argument proceeds in this way. It is true that the formal establishment of custom, as a law, depends on the will of the legislator.

[112] Michiels, *Normae Generales,* II, 71; Trummer, *Die Gewohnheit,* p. 125.

It is certain that his consent gives the legal bond. But it must not be forgotten that the people also play a part. By popular action a community anticipates the legislator and petitions him to give legal status to a certain mode of action. And thus the very acts of a community intend *by their nature* to establish a custom, even before a superior gives his consent.[113]

It has been objected to the position of Michiels that if the very nature of custom did not demand intention, countless optional acts would long ago have become obligatory. It might be claimed, for example, that the custom of daily Mass would bind all in many places and that the Angelus bell would sound a legal duty. This objection, however, does not seem to be valid, for clearly many practices, although good *ex devotione*, would be unreasonable and intolerable if they had to be shouldered by everybody under the burden of a legal obligation.

Although canonists are divided on the question whether intention flows from the nature of custom or from the will of the legislator, they are all agreed that the lawmaker demands its presence in a custom beside the law. It may be asked now how the community must express this intention. Need it be given in a clear definite manner or does a tacit manifestation of the will suffice? The will of the people need not be expressed. It may be found tacitly in the nature of the acts performed.[114] It is said that the nature of the acts rather shows the intent. This tacit will, of course, is not to be presumed easily, since people are not prone to undertake additional legal obligations. When actions have built up a certain prestige, so that contrary acts produce scandal or when especially, for example, a community adheres consistently to a difficult practice there would seem to be indication of an intention to produce customary law.

All canonists, therefore, conclude that in a custom beside the law there is need of intention. All likewise agree that this intention may be given tacitly and that it can often be found in the very nature of the acts.

[113] Van Hove, *De consuet.*, n. 129.

[114] Michiels, *Normae Generales*, II, 72; Van Hove, *De consuet.*, n. 130.

3. *The Question of Error in Custom Beside the Law*

When investigating the question of custom against the law it was seen that the silence of Canon 27 had given rise to various interpretations concerning error in custom against the law. Canon 28, however, in dealing with custom beside the law, clearly uses the word *scienter.*

The clearness of the law would seem to exclude all ignorance or error. The more common opinion is here adopted first of all by those who do not admit the possibility of reconciling error with an interpretative intention.[115] But others who will admit an interpretative intention in custom against the law will not admit it in the face of the wording *scienter* as found in the canon which treats of custom beside the law. These then join the camp of Michiels.[116]

Yet in spite of the text of the canon, the opinion is offered that *scienter* does not exclude all error for the whole prescribed time. It is suggested that the people cannot keep a practice for forty years, without the conviction arising that the acts are obligatory. At some time during so long a period the community would no longer have the intention of inducing custom and they would be in error concerning the legal obligation, which does not yet exist. Furthermore, since such customs supply law, rather than restrict liberty, it is fitting that they receive the consent of the ruler even when accompanied by error. The common good, as manifested in the popular action, should become customary law.[117] Once more this opinion must bring in the doctrine of the interpretative will to produce harmony between error and intention. Some canonists who admit such an intention in custom against the law will likewise admit it in custom beside the law.[118]

The more common opinion, therefore, refuses to admit error, when dealing with custom which supplies law, since the canon speaks so clearly of knowledge. Some, however, will accept what they call

[115] Michiels, *Normae Generales,* II, 75. *Cf. supra* 113.

[116] A Coronata, *Institutiones,* I, n. 42, note 4; Toso, *Comment. min.,* I. 85.

[117] Van Hove, *De consuet.,* n. 144.

[118] Cappello, *Summa,* I, n. 113; Cicognani, *Jus can.,* II, 171; Van Hove, *De consuet.,* n. 144.

error concomitans,[119] and they reconcile this presence of some error with the intention, which the word *animo* in the canon demands, by their doctrine of the interpretative will.

4. *The question of Good or Bad Faith in Custom Beside the Law*

There is hardly room for the question of good or bad faith in a custom beside the law. The community will always be in good faith when acting beside the law. For whether people observe a practice in ignorance, because they think they are bound thereto by a law, or whether they knowingly intend to create a law which does not exist, they will be in good faith in either hypothesis. The problem of good faith then does not present any difficulty at all in custom beside the law.

5. *Prescription in Custom Beside the Law*

Canon 28 contains the words *legitime praescripta,* which are worthy of note. The fact that this legislation, which concerns a custom beside the law, uses this term indicates that the prescription of custom is not in any way a real prescription, but a mere passage of time. This is the traditional doctrine and historically customs arising beside the law were not called "prescribed."

Before the codification of Canon Law the common opinion of canonists favored only ten years' duration for the prescription of custom beside the law, since that number of years was thought to constitute a *long* custom. The new legislation, however, demands a lapse of forty years for every custom, whether it be beside a universal or a particular law.

It has been noted [120] that in a custom against the law forty years' duration is not required if the legislator gives *special* consent. In custom beside the law, however, it is the opinion of some canonists that forty years' duration is always needed, even when the custom receives a special consent.[121]

[119] *Cf. supra* 111, 112, where the interpretative intention is studied.

[120] *Cf. supra* 117.

[121] Vermeersch-Creusen, *Epitome,* I, n. 138; Michiels, *Normae Generales,* II, 94. Cappello demands forty years if the special consent is only tacit and not expressed—*Summa,* I, n. 115.

They reason in this way. All law is either *lex* or *consuetudo*. The legislator of the Code has declared in what way each must be promulgated. For the promulgation of law (*lex*) the Code has adopted the method spoken of in Canon 9, the use of the magazine *Acta Apostolicae Sedis*. For the establishment of customary law there was much debate before the appearance of the Code, concerning the time needed for custom to introduce a law. The Code now clearly says that the legislator demands that a practice endure for forty years before it can become a law binding upon all. This opinion, therefore, argues that just as the will of a legislator institutes a law, when it is promulgated, so also he has chosen to institute customary law, when the people have petitioned him to legalize a forty years' practice. Prescribed time is the mode of promulgation for custom.

The reasoning of this opinion is logical enough, but it is gratuitous to assert that the canons on custom institute forty years as a mode of promulgation for the unwritten law. There is no basis for drawing the parallel between the promulgation of written law and the establishment of customary law.

There is no reason why a legislator cannot give special consent to a custom that introduces law, just as he can give such approval to a custom which abrogates law. Van Hove notes neatly that to deny special consent in custom beside the law is to prevent the *stylus curiae* from being established before forty years.[122]

Although it is said that forty years are not needed, when the special consent of the legislator is had, it does not follow that no duration of time is required for custom to introduce law. Custom originates in the succession of acts on the part of the people. It must be always remembered that the people begin the making of the law. This continuity and frequency of the acts has been investigated already, concerning custom against the law.[123] Unless there existed this popular action by a community to which the legislator gives his special consent, the law established could not be spoken of as customary law, but as *lex*, the law of the legislator alone.

[122] Van Hove, *De consuet.*, n. 196.

[123] *Cf. supra* 97.

6. *Is There Any Kind of Law Which Custom Cannot Introduce?*

It has been affirmed by some that custom cannot, for example, introduce new censures or irregularities.[124] Practically, it would not be easy for custom to produce an irregularity, but the wording of Canon 983 does not make this an impossibility.[125]

There seems to be no reason why custom cannot introduce even those laws called *irritantes vel inhabilitantes.* Because of express legislation, however, custom cannot create matrimonial impediments, for Canon 1041 clearly condemns as unreasonable any custom beside the law which attempts to introduce any new impediment.[126] It may be concluded, therefore, that apart from express reprobation by a legislator, a custom can introduce any kind of law.

Article 12. Custom Conformed to Law

Canon 29. Consuetudo est optima legum interpres.

The axiom that custom is the best interpreter of law has been handed down from the Roman Paulus, who says that if a question arises concerning the interpretation of law, we must look back to the law Rome used in such cases; for custom is the best expounder of the laws.[127] The value of custom in interpreting law might be considered under two aspects, as a practice which precedes a law canonizing that usage, or as a custom which refers to a law already enacted.

Popular usage might well influence a legislator, who is about to enact law. All things being considered, the lawmaker would act wisely to frame his statute in conformity with popular practice. A bishop, for example, noting that most of the parishes in his diocese observe a certain practice might in time reduce that practice to synodal law. In this sense it might well be said that custom is the best interpreter of law to be made.

[124] Cappello, *Summa,* I, n. 116.

[125] Nullum impedimentum perpetuum . . . nomine irregularitatis . . . contrahitur, nisi quod fuerit in canonibus qui sequuntur expressum (Canon 983).

[126] Consuetudo novum impedimentum inducens aut impedimentis existentibus contraria reprobatur (Canon 1041).

[127] D. (1, 3) 37; *cf. supra* 13, where Roman Law is treated.

Generally, however, the rule, enunciated in Canon 29, is understood of laws already formed and to these laws the axiom is applied that they are best interpreted by custom. One of the sources in the historical background of this canon is the letter of Pope Leo XIII, *Apostolicae Curae.* The matter referred to in that letter will help to illustrate the principle that custom is the best interpreter of law. The Pontiff took occasion to declare that ordinations administered according to the Anglican rite have been and are absolutely null and void. Some of the arguments used for this conclusion were based on the force of custom. It was pointed out that the Edwardine Ordinal used in England did not follow the *usual* form of the Church. There had been a departure from the established practice, said the letter, and it was pointed out that for three centuries the practice of reordaining converts from Anglicanism argued that the orders were considered null. There was ample evidence in pontifical documents to show the constant practice of the Church, and if there be any doubt concerning the enactments given in those documents, it is to be remembered that custom is the *optima legum interpres.* Since the Church has never had the practice of repeating ordination, the fact that the Apostolic See approved and sanctioned such a custom interprets the laws of past pontiffs.[128]

The law of which custom is the interpreter is either substantially clear or dubious. When a law is clear and the people carry it into action substantially they add no new obligation. Although the practice may add accidental modifications, on the whole it merely executes the duty imposed by the law. Popular usages corroborates the law and best shows the meaning which the legislator intended. In this situation then the custom is mere observance, a custom of fact. Since no new law is established none of the conditions mentioned throughout this study for the establishment of customary law are demanded.

On the other hand, if the law is doubtful, custom may again give a different kind of interpretation. The Roman Callistratus spoke of the value of custom in doubtful cases when he wrote that in doubtful cases which the law offers, the custom or the authority of things judged always in the same manner ought to have force of law.[129]

[128] Leo XIII, *litt. apost.*, 13 Sept., 1896—*Fontes* 631.

[129] D. (1, 3) 38; *cf. supra* 13.

It has been pointed out that Suarez was the first to notice the difference between custom which refers to a clear law and custom which applies to a doubtful law. Building on the fundamental difference in the two texts of Roman Law, canonists today say that when custom interprets a doubtful law it gives either a doctrinal or an authentic interpretation.[130]

The common usage gives a *doctrinal interpretation* only when it is not yet vested with all the conditions necessary to establish customary law. The mere observance of a community, which, for example, has not yet been legitimately prescribed, does not constitute a binding interpretation, a new legal obligation, but even while it is growing into a firm and certain interpretation it does give a prudent and safe rule for applying the meaning of the lawmaker.

This usual interpretation can establish the extension of the law's obligation. If it substantially restricts or extends the meaning of the law, the usage must be reduced to a custom either *contra* or *praeter legem.* If this interpretation extends over a period of forty years and has all the other conditions enumerated for customary law, then the interpretation is said to be *authentic* and it really induces a new obligation.[131]

The word *consuetudo,* then, in Canon 29 may be taken in two different meanings. First of all it may refer to a mere custom of fact, an observance which only executes a clear law, and neither adds nor subtracts from it substantially.[132] Secondly, the word may refer to a legal custom, which has assumed all the juridical characteristics of customary law, and which by adding a new objective norm is reduced to a custom either beside the law or against the law. But whether custom strictly executes a clear law, or adds a new obligation to a doubtful law, whether it be considered as custom of fact, or as custom of law, the axiom remains true that *consuetudo est optima legum interpres.*

[130] It may be noted that the word "authentic" will be used here not in the strict sense of Canon 17, but in the sense that it is an interpretation which the legislator will recognize.

[131] Cicognani, *Jus can.,* II, 173; Michiels, *Normae Generales,* II, 111; Cappello, *Summa,* I, n. 116; Van Hove, *De consuet.,* n. 243; A Coronata, *Inst.,* n. 43.

[132] *Cf.* Suarez, *supra* 64.

Article 13. The Abrogation of Custom

Canon 30. Firmo praescripto Can. 5, consuetudo contra legem vel praeter legem per contrariam consuetudinem aut legem revocatur, sed nisi expressam de iisdem mentionem fecerit, lex non revocat consuetudines centenarias aut immemorabiles, nec lex generalis consuetudines particulares.

Canon 5 provides for all customs which had sprung up before the Code and deals with their relation to the new law.[133] This canon treats of customs which may arise after the Code, whether they be against the law or beside it. A custom once established as law may be abolished either by another contrary custom or by a contrary law.

A. Abrogation of One Custom by Another Custom

1. That one custom may abrogate another it should be clear that a reconciliation is impossible (Canon 23). If the customs are really contrary one to the other, a question arises concerning the duration of time needed by the second custom. It is pointed out that Canon 30, which deals with the abrogation of customs, is silent concerning the time needed by one custom to abolish another. It is clear, however, that the legislator realizes that he has already provided for this in Canons 27 and 28, which treat of customs against the law and beside the law. Certainly the second custom must be considered as either *contra legem* or *praeter legem.*

If the first custom is held to be *contra legem,* the second contrary custom will be *praeter legem scriptam.* The bond of the old written law is considered abolished by the first custom. The second custom which is beside the written law, therefore, requires forty years' duration according to Canon 28.

If, on the other hand, the first custom is considered *praeter legem,* the second may be thought of as also *praeter legem* and from Canon 27 it needs forty years' duration.[134]

2. Some have maintained on the contrary that whether the prior custom is *contra* or *praeter legem,* the later contrary custom

[133] *Cf. supra* 73.

[134] Van Hove, *De consuet.,* n. 188.

must be held always as *contra legem consuetudinariam.*[135] But even if this be true it must be observed that Canon 27 reads *iuri ecclesiastico.* The term *iuri* is wider in its meaning than the expression *contra legem.* It includes both the written and customary law. Again, therefore, forty years must be considered the temporal norm for any custom to abolish a contrary custom. The import which this question had in the past [136] no longer exists, since the Code has established forty years as the time needed by all customs.

3. There is a final consideration. When the people have already established a custom, they may allow it to go into desuetude. The customary law then fades away and, as a matter of fact, there is a return to the old law. Some have argued that in this case only ten years' time is needed. This opinion is based on the arbitrary assumption that the lawmaker is pleased to have the people return to his old law and always wills the abandonment of custom. It presumes that he gives a tacit special consent.[137] It must not be forgotten, however, that an established custom is *law.* It has once received the approval of the legislator. It cannot be presumed arbitrarily then that he always wills a return to written law, since he once allowed a custom to become law. And, therefore, unless it can be established that a superior has given special consent, every custom must run the legal time of forty years, even the abrogation of customary law by desuetude.

B. Abrogation of Custom by Law

It is evident that one law may revoke another. Likewise a law may abolish a custom. It is clear also that the legislator can revoke any custom immediately by saying so expressly. This direct revocation presents no difficulty. A question arises, however, when a law is passed which only indirectly refers to contrary existing customs. In Canon 30, therefore, the legislator expresses certain principles which will explain his mind when a law seems to abrogate certain customs. Two kinds of laws must be considered here, a general law and a particular law, in their relation to customs.

[135] Michiels, *Normae Generales,* II, 115; Trummer, *Die Gewohnheit,* p. 191.

[136] *Cf. supra* 65.

[137] Wehrle, *De la coutume,* p. 417; A Coronata, *Institutiones,* I, n. 46.

1. *Abrogation by General Law*

The Code in Canon 30 says that a general law does not revoke particular customs unless it makes express mention of them. It likewise affirms that a general law does not revoke privileged customs which have attained the age called centenary or immemorial unless they are expressly mentioned.

The words *lex generalis* have provoked some discussion. What is a general law in the sense of Canon 30? Some claim that these words refer not alone to a law of the Code, or a universal law of the Church. For them the term has a wider meaning. A law, they argue, may be general without being universal. The law of a plenary council, they say, is general for a country; a provincial council makes laws which are general for a province. They, therefore, consider rather a juridical entity having within itself other lesser communities which are capable of introducing custom. Thus, for example, a province contains dioceses; a diocese contains parishes. This opinion then holds that the term *lex generalis* in Canon 30 is rather a relative term, that it applies to other than universal law, that it embraces any law of a larger community which is to be considered general in relation to the smaller communities within it.[138]

This doctrine which is a departure from the tradition of the canonists seems untenable. Canon 30 finds its source in the decretal of Pope Boniface, which applies to universal papal law. The traditional teaching of canonists has understood that decretal to apply to pontifical law. Even if the new opinion succeeds in creating a doubt, there is not sufficient reason to abandon the traditional interpretation (Canon 6, 4°). Furthermore, the principle behind Canon 30 is based on a presumption concerning the knowledge of a legislator. It is properly presumed that a universal lawmaker does not know every particular custom and, therefore, does not intend to legislate concerning them. But legislators of less general laws, such as bishops and religious superiors, are presumed to know the customs within their limited jurisdictions. It may be concluded, therefore, that the term *lex generalis* refers to a universal law.

[138] Trummer, *Die Gewohnheit,* p. 187.

The canon says then that universal law does not abolish particular customs contrary to the law, unless it expressly mentions them. A universal law does, however, revoke any general contrary custom which may exist. This is so because the legislator is thought to embrace all general customs in the scope of his law, since he can be presumed to have knowledge of these.

The canon implies secondly that a general law does not abrogate privileged customs which are one hundred years of age or immemorial, unless the law mentions them expressly. This is because the legislator is not presumed to abolish such venerable customs without definitely affirming so.

2. *Abrogation by Particular Law*

(a) If the particular law has been enacted by the Supreme Pontiff for a special place, it must be said that such a law abolishes *even general customs* which may be established in that place. This is effected even without mention of the custom since the legislator is presumed to know customs in a place for which he frames a particular law.

(b) But the particular law of a legislator, who is subordinate, does not abolish a *general* custom. Those who deny this, claim that Canon 30 gives the general rule that law can abolish custom, and the only restriction is placed on a general law.[189] Nevertheless the statement that a subordinate cannot abolish the general law must be maintained, since any interpretation of Canon 30 must yield to the principle that inferior legislators cannot act against the common law. And so, if perchance a general custom has been established with the consent of the Pope, the particular law of a bishop would not abrogate that custom, which has become general law.

(c) Particular customs, on the other hand, are revoked by a particular law, unless they be privileged. Whenever a custom depends upon the consent of a certain legislator for its establishment, a law enacted by the same person revokes the contrary custom. One opinion, however, goes so far as to suggest that a subordinate legislator

[189] A Coronata, *Institutiones,* I, n. 46.

cannot abrogate even a custom against his own law, because legal consent is granted to all qualified customs by the common law.[140] It should be remembered, however, that this legal consent is substituting, as it were, for the personal consent, which the legislator could give to any custom which refers to his law. Since his personal consent could establish a custom, so also his own law can abrogate it. And so, synodal law, for example, revokes contrary customs within the diocese.

(d) It is clear that a particular law revokes a particular custom which is established on the consent of the author of that law. But a further question remains to be investigated. What is the relationship of the particular law to customs which refer to the law of a superior?

It is affirmed on the one side that if a custom has been established by the consent of a superior legislator, the particular law of an inferior lawmaker would not abrogate the custom.[141] It is said that such a custom is outside the competency of the lesser legislator. According to this opinion, it would be difficult to see how a bishop, for example, could revoke within his diocese any custom against the Code.

More properly it should be maintained that the particular law of a subordinate legislator abrogates any particular custom which is founded on the *legal consent* of a legislative superior. This position can be established by an analysis of Canon 30. Let is be noted first of all that there is no question here of a custom which has received the *special* consent of a superior, because by such consent the customary law would be the special law of that legislator and no inferior could abrogate it. This question then concerns legal consent only. When a particular custom enjoys legal consent it assumes its force from the common law, which confirms all customs qualified with the necessary conditions. But the same common law gives even an inferior lawmaker power to enact particular laws. Canon 30 implies that law (any law) can revoke contrary custom. A qualification is then made concerning only privileged customs and a general law. From a study of this canon, then, it may be said, that a particular law, even of a subordinate, revokes a custom contrary to the law of a superior.

140 Toso, *Comment. min.*, I, 81, 82.

141 Michiels, *Normae Generales*, II, 123.

Synodal law, therefore, revokes customs established by legal consent against the Code, if they are flourishing in the diocese.[142]

It is clear that all centennial and immemorial customs are privileged against a particular law no less than against a general law. If they are to be abolished, they must be mentioned expressly.[143]

3. *Abrogating Clauses.*

Canon 30 says that express mention must be made of centennary and immemorial customs by any law and that a general law must mention particular customs if these are to be abolished. It may be asked now what is understood by express mention? If the custom is named specifically, which is seldom done, there is no difficulty. More often a phrase, known as an abrogating clause, is appended to the law. What is the effect of these abrogating clauses and in what sense do they constitute express mention?

Perhaps the most common phrase is *non obstante consuetudine contraria*. It may be affirmed that this formula does not constitute express mention. It would, therefore, include only general contrary customs and not particular or privileged customs.[144] The words *non obstante quacumque consuetudine* and *nulla obstante consuetudine* are considered to imply express mention of particular customs. But even these clauses are not held to include privileged customs, which have attained venerable age. Such must be named even more clearly by words like *etiam immemorabili vel centenaria*. The naming of these customs must be so exact, it is said, that even the clause *non obstante consuetudine centenaria* does not include an immemorial custom.[145]

If the legislator in his condemnation assigns certain reasons why he has condemned contrary customs, it seems clear that every custom, of any age, which embodies those reasons is included in the con-

142 Vermeersch-Creusen, *Epitome*, n. 143.

143 Michiels, *Normae Generales*, II, 122; Trummer, *Die Gewohnheit*, p. 188.

144 Vermeersch-Creusen, *Epitome*, I, n. 143; Ojetti, *Comment.*, I, 120.

145 Vermeersch-Creusen, *Epitome*, I, n. 143; *cf.* Pius XI, *Constitutio Apostolica, Deus Scientiarum Dominus*, 24 May, 1931, art. 58—*AAS*, XXIII (1931), 262.

demnation. Every custom is likewise condemned, when the clause expressly names one or more customs which it excepts.[146]

These clauses, which revoke custom, are not the same as reprobatory clauses. They do not condemn the custom as unreasonable, and the practice may revive in the future.[147]

Article 14. The Proof of Custom

The second title of the first book of the Code says nothing of the proof that might be needed to vindicate the existence of custom. It has been claimed that custom is a law, a juridical norm. When this law is known to a judge there is no need of proof and the judge should apply the law even as he would the written law.[148]

On the other hand it should be noted that custom and statute law are not identical. It is comparatively easy to prove the existence of the written law, but customary law, which is not notorious, is not always evident. It may be admitted that custom which, in the meaning of the law, is notorious needs no proof (Canon 1747, 1°). But it should not be left to the judge to determine alone the existence of custom, which is not notorious. There is no doubt that an established custom has force of law, but what must be proved is the fact of its establishment.[149]

If proof should be necessary the burden falls upon the shoulders of the party who cites the custom. The title of the Code which deals with custom is wisely silent concerning this question. If proof should be needed, the procedure is amply provided for in the fourth book of the Code, more particularly in Title X, *De probationibus*.

[146] Michiels, *Normae Generales*, II, 120.

[147] Cappello, *Summa*, I, n. 121; Trummer, *Die Gewohnheit*, p. 155; Cicognani, *Jus can.*, II, 175.

[148] Michiels, *Normae Generales*, II, 100.

[149] Cappello, *Summa*, I, n. 120; Roberti, *De processibus*, I, n. 277; Ojetti, *Comment.*, I, 169; Cicognani, *Jus can.*, II, 159; Noval, *Comment.*, lib. IV, n. 440.

BIBLIOGRAPHY

Sources

Acta Apostolicae Sedis, Romae, 1909-

Acta Sanctae Sedis, 41 vols., Romae, 1865-1908.

Concilia Provincialia Baltimori Habita, 1829-1849, 2. ed., Baltimore, 1851.

Concilii Plenarii Baltimorensis II, Acta et Decreta, Baltimorae, 1868.

Concilii Plenarii Baltimorensis III, Acta et Decreta, Baltimorae, 1886.

Canones et Decreta Concilii Tridentini, ed. Richter-Schulte, Lipsiae, 1853.

Codex Juris Canonici, Pii X Pontificis Maximi jussu digestus, Benedicti Papae XV auctoritate promulgatus, Romae, 1918.

Codicis Juris Canonici Fontes, cura Emi. Petri Card. Gasparri editi, 7 vols., Romae, 1922-1935.

Corpus Juris Canonici, editio Lipsiensis Secunda post Aemilii Richteri curas . . . instruxit Aemilius Friedburg, 2 vols., Lipsiae, 1922.

Corpus Juris Civilis, Vol. I, *Institutiones*—recognovit P. Krueger; Vol. II, *Codex Justianus*—recognovit et retractavit P. Krueger; Vol. III, *Novellae Constitutiones*—R. Schoell; opus Schoelli morte interceptum absolvit G. Kroll, Berolini, 1928-1929.

Decreta Authentica Congregationis Sacrorum Rituum, 7 vols., Romae, 1898-

Harduin, Jean, *Acta Conciliorum et Epistolae Decretales ac Constitutiones Summorum Pontificum*, 12 vols., Parisiis, 1715.

Mansi, J. D., *Sacrorum Conciliorum Nova et Amplissima Collectio*, 58 vols., Arnheim, 1901-1927.

Migne, P. J., *Patrologiae Cursus Completus*—Series Latina, 221 vols., Parisiis, 1844-1855; Series Graeca, 161 vols., Parisiis, 1857-1866.

Sacrae Romanae Rotae Decisiones seu Sententiae, 8 vols., and appendix, Romae, 1761.

Reference Works

Andreae, Joannes, *Commentaria novella in Decretales Gregorii IX*, Venetiis, 1612. Appendix de consuetudine ad L. I, tit. 4.

(Bachofen), Charles Augustine, *A Commentary on the New Code of Canon Law*, 4. ed., 8 vols., St. Louis, 1921-1929.

Bauduin, Gulielmus, *De consuetudine in iure canonico*, Lovanii, 1888.

Benedictus XIV, *De Synodo Dioecesana*, 2 vols., Romae, 1806.

Biagio, Brugio, *Istitutzioni di Diritto Romano*, Torino, Unione Tipografico-Editrice Torinese, 1926.

Biondi, Biondo, *Corso di Istitutzioni di Diritto Romano*, Vol. I, 1929.

Blat, Alberto, *Commentarium Textus Codicis Juris Canonici*, Romae, Ex Typographia Pontificia in Instituto Pii IX, 1921.

Bonfante Pietro, *Rivista di diritto commerciale*, Milano, 1904.

Bouscaren, T. L., *The Canon Law Digest*, Milwaukee, 1934.

Bernard of Botone (Botonius), *Apparatus ad Decretales Gregorii IX*, L. I, tit. 4, c. 11.

Bouix, Marie Dominique, *Tractatus de principiis iuris canonici*, 3. ed., Vol. I, Parisiis, 1882.

Brie, S., *Die Lehre vom Gewohnheitsrecht*, Breslavia, 1889.

Butrius, Antonius, *Pars prima super primo Decretalium*, Lugduni, 1555; L. I, tit. 4, c. 11, Repetitio.

Cappello, F. M., *Summa Juris Canonici*, I, Romae, Apud. Aedes Universitatis Gregorianae, 1928.

Chelodi, J., *Jus de Personis*, 2. ed., Tridenti, 1927.

Cicognani, A. G., *Jus Canonicum*, 2 vols., Romae, Ex Officina Typographica Ausonia, 1925.

Clark, E. C., *Roman Private Law*, Cambridge, University Press, 1914.

Cocchi, G., *Commentarium in Codicem Juris Canonici*, 7 vols., Taurini, Marietti, 1925-1931.

Conte A Coronata, M., *Institutiones Juris Canonici*, I, Taurini, ex Officina Libraria Marietti, 1928.

Curtius, Rochus, *De consuetudine, in Tractatus illustrium in utraque iuris facultate iurisconsultorum*, Venetiis, 1584-1585.

D'Angelo, Sosius, *Jus Digestorum*, Vol. I, Romae, Lega Italiana Catholica Editrice, 1927.

Ferrini, Contardo, *Pandette*, Romae, Societá Editrice Libraria, 1927.

Flumene, F., *La consuetudine nel suo valore giuridico*, Sassari, 1925.

Geny, F., *Méthode d'interpretation et sources en droit privé*, Paris, 1919.

Giacchi, Orio, *Della dottrina della interpretazione*, Milano, Societá Editrice "Vita et Pensiero," 1935.

Gousset, Thomas, *Exposition des Principes Du Droit Canonique*, Paris, 1859.

Hostiensis (Henricus de Segusio), *Apparatus super quinque libros Decretalium; Summa Aurea*. Lugduni, 1568.

Kreutzwald, P. C. A., *De canonica iuris consuetudinarii praescriptione*, Friburgi Brisigavorum, 1873.

Laymann, P., *Theologia Moralis*, Monachii, 1625.

Michiels, Gommarus, *Normae Generales Juris Canonici*, 2 vols., Lublin-Polonia. Universitas Catholica, 1929.

Maroto, Philippus, *Institutiones Juris Canonici*, 2 vols., Romae, 1921.

Ojetti, Benedictus, *Commentarium in Codicem Juris Canonici*, 3 vols., Romae apud Aedes Universitatis Gregorianae, 1927.

Pacchioni, Giovanni, *Corso di Diritto Romano*, Torino, Unione Tipografico-Editrice Torinese, 1918.

Panormitanus (Nicholas de Tudeschis), *Commentaria*, 8 vols., Venetiis, 1588.

Phillips, George, *Kirchenrecht*, III, Regensburg, 1850; French translation by J. P. Crouzet, Paris, 1855.

Pirhing, Ernrico, *Ius Canonicum in V Libros Decretalium distributum*, Venetiis, 1759.

Puchta, G. F., *Das Gewohnheitsrecht*, 2 vols., Erlangen, 1828-1837.

Reiffenstuel, Anacletus, *Ius Canonicum Universum*, 7 vols., Parisiis, 1864-1870.

Sägmüller, J. B., *Lehrbuch des Katholischen Kirchenrects*, 4. ed., Berlin, Freiburg-im-Breisgau, 1926.

Savigny, Frederick V. von, *System des Heutigen römischen Rechts*, Berlin, 1840-1849.

Schmalzgrueber, Franciscus, *Jus Ecclesiasticum Universum*, 12 vols., Romae, 1843-1845.

Schulte, J. F., *Das katholische Kirchenrecht*, I, Giessen, 1860.

Suarez, Franciscus, *Opera Omnia*, 26 vols., Parisiis, 1856-1861.

Thomas Aquinas, *Summa Theologica*, ed. 2, Romana, Romae, 1894.

Toso, A., *Ad Codicem iuris canonici Commentaria minora*, I, Romae, 1921, Tiferni Tiberini, Ex Offic. Typogr. Vinciana.

Trummer, Josef, *Die Gewohnheit als kirckliche Rechtsquelle*, Wien, Mayer & Co., 1932.

Van Hove, A., *Normae Generales*, Mechliniae-Romae, H. Dessain, 1930; *De Consuetudine*, 1933.

Vermeersch, A.-Creusen, J., *Epitome Juris Canonici*, 4.-5. ed., 3 vols., Mechliniae, 1931-1933.

Wehrlé, Rene, *De la coutume dans le droit canonique. Essai historique s'étendant des origines de l'Église au pontificat de Pie XI*, Paris, Sirey, 1928.

Wernz, F. X., *Jus Decretalium*, 3. ed., Vol. I, Romae, 1913.

Windscheid, B., *Lehrbuch des Pandektenrechts*, Francfurt, 1891.

Zallinger, Jacobus, *Institutiones Iuris Ecclesiastici Maxime Privati Ordine Decretalium*, I, Romae. Typis Antonii Bouzaler, 1823.

PERIODICALS

American Ecclesiastical Review, Philadelphia, 1889-

Bullettino dell' instituto di Diritto Romano, Romae, 1891-

Homiletic and Pastoral Review, The, New York, 1900-

Irish Ecclesiastical Record, Dublin, 1864-

Jus Pontificium, Romae, 1921-

Le Canoniste Contemporain, Paris, 1881-1926.

Periodica de Re Morali, Canonica, Liturgica, Romae, 1905-

Zeitschrift für katholische Theologie, Innsbruck, 1877-

Zeitschrift de Savigny Stiftung—Römische Abteilung, Weimar, 1880-
Kanonistische Abteilung, Weimar, 1911-

ALPHABETICAL INDEX

VITA

Merlin Joseph Guilfoyle was born July 15, 1908, at San Francisco, California, and attended St. James' Grammar School in that city. In 1922 he entered St. Patrick's Minor Seminary, Menlo Park, California, and was subsequently transferred to St. Joseph's Preparatory Seminary, Mountain View, California. He returned to St. Patrick's Major Seminary and was ordained to the priesthood June 10, 1933. In September, 1934, he entered the Catholic University of America to pursue a graduate course of studies in the School of Canon Law, from which he received the Baccalaureate in Canon Law in June, 1934, and the Licentiate the following June.

CANON LAW STUDIES

1. FRERIKS, REV. CELESTINE A., C.PP.S., J.C.D., Religious Congregations in Their External Relations, 121 pp., 1916.
2. GALLIHER, REV. DANIEL M., O.P., J.C.D., Canonical Elections, 117 pp., 1917.
3. BORKOWSKI, REV. AURELIUS L., O.F.M., J.C.D., De Confraternitatibus Ecclesiasticis, 136 pp., 1918.
4. CASTILLO, REV. CAYO, J.C.D., Disertacion Historico-Canonica sobre la Potestad del Cabildo en Sede Vacante o Impedida del Vicario Capitular, 99 pp., 1919 (1918).
5. KUBELBECK, REV. WILLIAM J., S.T.B., J.C.D., The Sacred Penitentiaria and Its Relation to Faculties of Ordinaries and Priests, 129 pp., 1918.
6. PETROVITS, REV. JOSEPH, J.C., S.T.D., J.C.D., The New Church Law on Matrimony, X-461 pp., 1919.
7. HICKEY, REV. JOHN J., S.T.B., J.C.D., Irregularities and Simple Impediments in the New Code of Canon Law, 100 pp., 1920.
8. KLEKOTKA, REV. PETER J., S.T.B., J.C.D., Diocesan Consultors, 179 pp., 1920.
9. WANENMACHER, REV. FRANCIS, J.C.D., The Evidence in Ecclesiastical Procedure Affecting the Marriage Bond, 1920 (Printed 1935).
10. GOLDEN, REV. HENRY FRANCIS, J.C.D., Parochial Benefices in the New Code, IV-119 pp., 1921 (Printed 1925).
11. KOUDELKA, REV. CHARLES J., J.C.D., Pastors, Their Rights and Duties According to the New Code of Canon Law, 211 pp., 1921.
12. MELO, REV. ANTONIUS, O.F.M., J.C.D., De Exemptione Regularium, X-188 pp., 1921.
13. SCHAAF, REV. VALENTINE THEODORE, O.F.M., S.T.B., J.C.D., The Cloister, X-180 pp., 1921.
14. BURKE, REV. THOMAS JOSEPH, S.T.D., J.C.D., Competence in Ecclesiastical Tribunals, IV-117 pp., 1922.
15. LEECH, REV. GEORGE LEO, J.C.D., A Comparative Study of the Constitution "Apostolicae Sedis" and the "Codex Juris Canonici," 179 pp., 1922.
16. MOTRY, REV. HUBERT LOUIS, S.T.D., J.C.D., Diocesan Faculties According to the Code of Canon Law, II-167 pp., 1922.
17. MURPHY, REV. GEORGE LAWRENCE, J.C.D., Delinquencies and Penalties in The Administration and the Reception of the Sacraments, IV-121 pp., 1923.
18. O'REILLY, REV. JOHN ANTHONY, S.T.B., J.C.D., Ecclesiastical Sepulture in the New Code of Canon Law, II-129 pp., 1923.
19. MICHALICKA, REV. WENCESLAS CYRILL, O.S.B., J.C.D., Judicial Procedure in Dismissal of Clerical Exempt Religious, 107 pp., 1923.

20. Dargin, Rev. Edward Vincent, S.T.B., J.C.D., Reserved Cases According to the Code of Canon Law, IV-103 pp., 1924.
21. Godfrey, Rev. John A., S.T.B., J.C.D., The Right of Patronage According to the Code of Canon Law, 153 pp., 1924.
22. Hagedorn, Rev. Francis Edward, J.C.D., General Legislation on Indulgences, II-154 pp., 1924.
23. King, Rev. James Ignatius, J.C.D., The Administration of the Sacraments to Dying Non-Catholics, V-141 pp., 1924.
24. Winslow, Rev. Francis Joseph, O.F.M., J.C.D., Vicars and Prefects Apostolic, IV-149 pp., 1924.
25. Correa, Rev. Jose Servelion, S.T.L., J.C.D., La Potestad Legislativa de la Iglesia Catolica, IV-127 pp., 1925.
26. Dugan, Rev. Henry Francis, A.M., J.C.D., The Judiciary Department of the Diocesan Curia, 87 pp., 1925.
27. Keller, Rev. Charles Frederick, S.T.B., J.C.D., Mass Stipends, 167 pp., 1925.
28. Paschang, Rev. John Linus, J.C.D., The Sacramentals According to the Code of Canon Law, 129 pp., 1925.
29. Pointek, Rev. Cyrillus, O.F.M., S.T.B., J.C.D., De Indulto Exclaustrationis necnon Saecularizationis, XIII-289 pp., 1925.
30. Kearney, Rev. Richard Joseph, S.T.B., J.C.D., Sponsors at Baptism According to the Code of Canon Law, IV-127 pp., 1925.
31. Bartlett, Rev. Chester Joseph, A.M., LL.B., J.C.D., The Tenure of Parochial Property in the United States of America, V-108 pp., 1926.
32. Kilker, Rev. Adrian Jerome, J.C.D., Extreme Unction, V-425 pp., 1926.
33. McCormick, Rev. Robert Emmett, J.C.D., Confessors of Religious, VIII-266 pp., 1926.
34. Miller, Rev. Newton Thomas, J.C.D., Founded Masses According to the Code of Canon Law, VII-93 pp., 1926.
35. Roelker, Rev. Edward G., S.T.D., J.C.D., Principles of Privilege According to the Code of Canon Law, XI-166 pp., 1926.
36. Bakalarczyk, Rev. Richardus, M.I.C., J.U.D., De Novitiatu, VIII-208 pp., 1927.
37. Pizzuti, Rev. Lawrence, O.F.M., J.U.L., De Parochis Religiosis, 1927. (Not Printed.)
38. Bliley, Rev. Nicholas Martin, O.S.B., J.C.D., Altars According to the Code of Canon Law, XIX-132 pp., 1927.
39. Brown, Mr. Brendan Francis, A.B., LL.M., J.U.D., The Canonical Juristic Personality with Special Reference to its Status in the United States of America, V-212 pp., 1927.
40. Cavanaugh, Rev. William Thomas, C.P., J.U.D., The Reservation of the Blessed Sacrament, VIII-101 pp., 1927.
41. Doheny, Rev. William J., C.S.C., A.B., J.U.D., Church Property: Modes of Acquisition, X-118 pp., 1927.
42. Feldhaus, Rev. Aloysius H., C.PP.S., J.C.D., Oratories, IX-141 pp., 1927.

43. KELLY, REV. JAMES PATRICK, A.B., J.C.D., The Jurisdiction of the Simple Confessor, X-208 pp., 1927.
44. NEUBERGER, REV. NICHOLAS J., J.C.D., Canon 6 or the Relation of the Codex Juris Canonici to the Preceding Legislation, V-95 pp. 1927.
45. O'KEEFE, REV. GERALD MICHAEL, J.C.D., Matrimonial Dispensations, Powers of Bishops, Priests, and Confessors, VIII-232 pp., 1927.
46. QUIGLEY, REV. JOSEPH A. M., A.B., J.C.D., Condemned Societies, 139 pp., 1927.
47. ZAPLOTNIK, REV. JOHANNES LEO, J.C.D., De Vicariis Foraneis, X-142 pp., 1927.
48. DUSKIE, REV. JOHN ALOYSIUS, A.B., J.C.D., The Canonical Status of the Orientals in the United States, VIII-196 pp., 1928.
49. HYLAND, REV. FRANCIS EDWARD, J.C.D., Excommunication, Its Nature, Historical Development and Effects, VIII-181 pp., 1928.
50. REINMANN, REV. GERALD JOSEPH, O.M.C., J.C.D., The Third Order Secular of Saint Francis, 201 pp., 1928.
51. SCHENK, REV. FRANCIS J., J.C.D., The Matrimonial Impediments of Mixed Religion and Disparity of Cult, XVI-318 pp., 1929.
52. COADY, REV. JOHN JOSEPH, S.T.D., J.U.D., A.M., The Appointment of Pastors, VIII-150 pp., 1929.
53. KAY, REV. THOMAS HENRY, J.C.D., Competence in Matrimonial Procedure, VIII-164 pp., 1929.
54. TURNER, REV. SIDNEY JOSEPH, C.P., J.U.D., The Vow of Poverty, XLIX-217 pp., 1929.
55. KEARNEY, REV. RAYMOND A., A.B., S.T.D., J.C.D., The Principles of Delegation, VII-149 pp., 1929.
56. CONRAN, REV. EDWARD JAMES, A.B., J.C.D., The Interdict, V-163 pp., 1930.
57. O'NEIL, REV. WILLIAM H., J.C.D., Papal Rescripts of Favor, VII-218 pp., 1930.
58. BASTNAGEL, REV. CLEMENT VINCENT, J.U.D., The Appointment of Parochial Adjutants and Assistants, XV-257 pp., 1930.
59. FERRY, REV. WILLIAM A., A.B., J.C.D., Stole Fees, V-136, pp., 1930.
60. COSTELLO, REV. JOHN MICHAEL, A.B., J.C.D., Domicile and Quasi-Domicile, VII-201 pp., 1930.
61. KREMER, REV. MICHAEL NICHOLAS, A.B., S.T.B., J.C.D., Church Support in the United States, VI-136 pp., 1930.
62. ANGULO, REV. LUIS, C.M., J.C.D., Legislation de la Iglesia sobre la intencion en la application de la Santa Misa, VII-104 pp., 1931.
63. FREY, REV. WOLFGANG, NORBERT, O.S.B., A.B., J.C.D., The Act of Religious Profession, VIII-174 pp., 1931.
64. ROBERTS, REV. JAMES BRENDAN, A.B., J.C.D., The Banns of Marriage, XIV-140 pp., 1931.
65. RYDER, REV. RAYMOND ALOYSIUS, A.B., J.C.D., Simony, IX-151 pp., 1931.

66. CAMPAGNA, REV. ANGELO, PH.D., J.U.D., Il Vicario Generale del Vescovo, VII-205 pp., 1931.
67. COX, REV. JOSEPH GODFREY, A.B., J.C.D., The Administration of Seminaries, VI-124 pp., 1931.
68. GREGORY, REV. DONALD J., J.U.D., The Pauline Privilege, XV-165 pp., 1931.
69. DONOHUE, REV. JOHN F., J.C.D., The Impediment of Crime, VII-110 pp., 1931.
70. DOOLEY, REV. EUGENE A., O.M.I., J.C.D., Church Law on Sacred Relics, IX-143 pp., 1931.
71. ORTH, REV. CLEMENT RAYMOND, O.M.C., J.C.D., The Approbation of Religious Institutes, 171 pp., 1931.
72. PERNICONE, REV. JOSEPH M., A.B., J.C.D., The Ecclesiastical Prohibition of Books, XII-267 pp., 1932.
73. CLINTON, REV. CONNELL, A.B., J.C.D., The Paschal Precept, IX-108 pp., 1932.
74. DONNELLY, REV. FRANCIS B., A.M., S.T.L., J.C.D., The Diocesan Synod, VIII-125 pp., 1932.
75. TORRENTE, REV. CAMILO, C.M.F., J.C.D., Las Processiones Sagradas, V-145 pp., 1932.
76. MURPHY, REV. EDWIN J., C.PP.S., J.C.D., Suspension Ex Informata Conscientia, XI-122 pp., 1932.
77. MACKENZIE, REV. ERIC F., A.M., S.T.L., J.C.D., The Delict of Heresy in its Commission, Penalization, Absolution, VII-124 pp., 1932.
78. LYONS, REV. AVITUS E., S.T.B., J.C.D., The Collegiate Tribunal of First Instance, XI-147 pp., 1932.
79. CONNOLLY, REV. THOMAS A., J.C.D., Appeals, XI-195, pp., 1932.
80. SANGMEISTER, REV. JOSEPH V., A.B., J.C.D., Force and Fear as Precluding Matrimonial Consent, V-211, pp., 1932.
81. JAEGER, REV. LEO A., A.B., J.C.D., The Administration of Vacant and Quasi-Vacant Episcopal Sees in the United States, IX-229 pp., 1932.
82. RIMLINGER, REV. HERBERT T., J.C.D., Error Invalidating Matrimonial Consent, VII-79 pp., 1932.
83. BARRETT, REV. JOHN D. M., S.S., J.C.D., A Comparative Study of the Third Plenary Council of Baltimore and the Code, IX-221 pp., 1932.
84. CARBERRY, REV. JOHN J., PH.D., S.T.D., J.C.D., The Juridical Form of Marriage, X-177 pp., 1934.
85. DOLAN, REV. JOHN L., A.B., J.C.D., The Defensor Vinculi, XII, 157 pp., 1934.
86. HANNAN, REV. JEROME D., A.M., S.T.D., LL.B., J.C.D., The Canon Law of Wills, IX-517 pp., 1934.
87. LEMIEUX, REV. DELISLE A., A.M., J.C.D., The Sentence in Ecclesiastical Procedure, IX-131 pp., 1934.
88. O'ROURKE, REV. JAMES J., A.B., J.C.D., Parish Registers, VII-109 pp., 1934.

89. TIMLIN, REV. BARTHOLOMEW, O.F.M., A.M., J.C.D., Conditional Matrimonial Consent, X-381 pp., 1934.
90. WAHL, REV. FRANCIS X., A.B., J.C.D., The Matrimonial Impediments of Consanguinity and Affinity, VI-125 pp., 1934.
91. WHITE, REV. ROBERT J., A.B., LL.B., S.T.B., J.C.D., Canonical Ante-Nuptial Promises and the Civil Law, VI-152 pp., 1934.
92. HERRERA, REV. ANTONIO PARRA, O.C.D., J.C.D., Legislacion Ecclesiastica sobra el Ayuno y la Abstinencia, XI-191 pp., 1935.
93. KENNEDY, REV. EDWIN J., J.C.D., The Special Matrimonial Process in Cases of Evident Nullity, X-165 pp., 1935.
94. MANNING, REV. JOHN J., A.B., J.C.D., Presumption of Law in Matrimonial Procedure, XI-111 pp., 1935.
95. MOEDER, REV. JOHN M., J.C.D., The Proper Bishop for Ordination and Dimissorial Letters, VII-135 pp., 1935.
96. O'MARA, REV. WILLIAM A., A.B., J.C.D., Canonical Causes for Matrimonial Dispensations, IX-155 pp., 1935.
97. REILLY, REV. PETER, J.C.D., Residence of Pastors, IX-81 pp., 1935.
98. SMITH, REV. MARINER T., O.P., S.T.Lr., J.C.D., The Penal Law for Religious, VII-169 pp., 1935.
99. WHALEN, REV. DONALD W., A.M., J.C.D., The Value of Testimonial Evidence in Matrimonial Procedure, XIII-297 pp., 1935.
100. CLEARY, REV. JOSEPH F., J.C.D., Canonical Limitations on the Alienation of Church Property, VIII-141 pp., 1936.
101. GLYNN, REV. JOHN C., J.C.D., The Promoter of Justice, XX-337 pp., 1936.
102. BRENNAN, REV. JAMES H., S.S., M.A., S.T.B., J.C.L., The Simple Convalidation of Marriage.
103. BRUNINI, REV. JOSEPH BERNARD, J.C.L., The Clerical Obligations of Canons 139 and 142.
104. CONNOR, REV. MAURICE, A.B., J.C.L., The Administrative Removal of Pastors.
105. GUILFOYLE, REV. MERLIN JOSEPH, J.C.L., Custom.
106. HUGHES, REV. JAMES AUSTIN, A.B., A.M., J.C.L., Witnesses in Criminal Trials of Clerics.
107. JANSEN, REV. RAYMOND J., A.B., S.T.L., J.C.L., Canonical Provisions for Catechetical Instruction.
108. KEALY, REV. JOHN JAMES, A.B., J.C.L., The Introductory Libellus in Church Court Procedure.
109. MCMANUS, REV. JAMES EDWARD, C.SS.R., J.C.L., The Administration of Temporal Goods in Religious Institutes.
110. MORIARITY, REV. EUGENE JAMES, J.C.L., Oaths in Ecclesiastical Courts.
111. RAINER, REV. ELIGIUS GEORGE, C.SS.R., J.C.L., Suspension of Clerics.
112. REILLY, REV. THOMAS F., C.SS.R., J.C.L., Visitation of Religious.

www.ingramcontent.com/pod-product-compliance
Lightning Source LLC
LaVergne TN
LVHW050225080826
844660LV00012B/469

9780813222943